Etudes for Piano Teachers

Etudes
for
Piano
Teachers

Reflections on the Teacher's Art

STEWART GORDON

New York   Oxford
OXFORD UNIVERSITY PRESS
1995

Oxford University Press

Oxford   New York   Toronto
Delhi   Bombay   Calcutta   Madras   Karachi
Kuala Lumpur   Singapore   Hong Kong   Tokyo
Nairobi   Del es Salaam   Cape Town
Melbourne   Auckland   Madrid

and associated companies in
Berlin   Ibadan

Published by Oxford University Press, Inc.,

198 Madison Avenue, New York, New York 10016-4314

Oxford is a registered trademark of Oxford University Press

The source material for this book appeared from June 1973 through January 1982
as a column entitled "The New Davidites" in *American Music Teacher*,
the official journal of Music Teachers National Association.

Library of Congress Cataloging in Publication Data
Gordon, Stewart, 1930–
Etudes for piano teachers:
reflections on the teacher's art /
Stewart Gordon.
p.   cm.   Includes index.
ISBN 0-19-509322-4
1. Piano — Instruction and study.
I. Title.
MT220.G67   1995   786.2'193'071—dc20   94-25597

9 8 7 6 5 4 3

Printed in the United States of America
on acid-free paper

To Today's New Davidites —
that is,
to those who love the piano,
who love teaching the piano,
and who will fight to see that the wonderful tradition
of piano playing and teaching will live on in our society.

Preface

Between the fall of 1973 and the beginning of 1982, a series of twenty-seven pedagogical articles appeared in the *American Music Teacher* under the heading of "The New Davidites." Borrowing the symbolism used by Robert Schumann in the *Neue Zeitschrift für Musik* in the early nineteenth century, I wrote on subjects which ranged over a variety of topics from perennial concerns of teaching, such as practice procedures and memorizing, to more topical ones, such as current directions in which the profession seemed to be headed and the kind of students and musicians our society seemed to be spawning.

The end of the series took place at about the same time I terminated my piano editorship of the *American Music Teacher*, for I had embarked on a decade of turning my career in the direction of higher-education administration. In the years that followed, many professional teachers not only indicated that they had found "New Davidites" useful and helpful, but also that they had saved and copied them for continued use, often sharing them with their students. It was this enthusiasm which gave me the impetus for the present volume of essays.

Most of "The New Davidites" are all here, revised and updated to reflect my more recent thinking, and often augmented for more clarity and completeness. To the original articles are added more than half a dozen new essays which are born of my own return in 1987 to my first love, that of being a full-time musician with most of my activities focused on teaching the piano and its literature in the studio and the classroom.

My own love for the art and profession of piano teaching has inspired the only possible dedication of this volume.

Los Angeles   S. G.
June 1994

Contents

Part III. Transcendental Studies

Part I

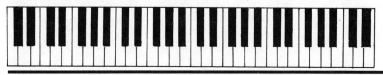

Fundamental Studies

1

Recognition Patterns

Teaching and Performing

S UPERLATIVE teaching is an achievement in any field; it is perhaps even harder to achieve in the field of music, where so much depends on unwritten tradition, elusive style characteristics, and abstract concepts. The teaching of the art of music should be regarded as having at least equal status with the art of performing music, and the proposition might even be argued that a career in which teaching is an important component makes more lasting contributions to society than one centered only on performance.

The fact remains, moreover, that most professional musicians are going to be heavily involved in both teaching and performing, and over 95 percent of them are going to depend on teaching as the mainstay of their professional income. Thus it remains a mystery why, by some strange compulsion, we, as a profession of practitioners and teachers, persist in subscribing to concepts which suggest that performers and teachers are musicians of separate traditions, requiring different programs of preparation. We often even categorize aptitudes and gifts to the extent that we suggest a choice must be made either to teach or to perform. Moreover, if performers of recognized stature persist in having students, such activity is regarded as "teaching performance," as opposed to others who "teach pedagogy."

Once having established a house divided, many of us then worry about the fact that "performers," who by the nature of their activity garner an admiring public, are accorded first-class citizenship in our profession while "teachers" must remain, if not totally unappreciated, at least unheralded and long suffering. Continued belief in this division gives rise to belittling homilies such as, "If you can't perform, you can always teach" or "Those who can, do; those who can't, teach." On the other side of the coin are comments which describe stereotypes who "play well, but are unable to teach" or, on a more subtle level, who "do nothing but coach," implying lack of ability to teach beyond the level of exhorting imitation.

Like most deep-seated prejudice, these viewpoints gain their vitality from half-truths and distortions of reality. Those who believe them can, indeed, point to examples to prove such contentions. But such examples are often exaggerated and simply reflect the obvious facts that we are not all gifted in the same ways; we cannot care with equal passion about all aspects of our profession; and there is not enough time for most of us to pursue even those things we are passionate about. Indeed, choices do have to be made. We besmirch our professional self-esteem, however, by assuming such choices are made only as a result of an aptitude deficiency, poor market conditions, or being just plain unlucky. Rather, we need to learn to assume such choices are made as a result of vision, talent, and love. Perhaps the most insidious manifestation of pitting "performance" and "pedagogy" against each other is the impact such thinking has on the generation of young musicians who aspire to become professionals. Teaching generally comes off second best. Many young musicians come to regard teaching as a by-product of their musical activity during their years of preparation: a useful, convenient, money-making by-product requiring only the time necessary to give the lessons, but not too much more.

Typically the young person turns to teaching as a way of earning a little extra money during the time of receiving his or her own professional training. A few beginners are taken on a private basis; or if the young person is on the college level, an affiliation with a commercial music store or studio may be forged, the young person teaching at an hourly rate whomever is provided. Such teaching may not be very knowledgeable or very forceful at this stage of a young person's career, but it is probably seldom very harmful and indeed often provides a beneficial way of imparting rudiments to beginning students.

In turn the young person gains experience in teaching and, as professional training continues, begins to see his or her own teacher's work from a pedagogical viewpoint, undoubtedly incorporating many of that teacher's principles and methods along the way. This kind of apprenticeship is a time-honored way of passing knowledge and practice from generation to generation, particularly in the arts and crafts. This system might be improved upon, but it has probably operated from the dawn of civilization, is fairly effective, and will undoubtedly be around for a long time.

Young musicians who are studying at institutions which offer course work in pedagogy may be able to integrate their images of performing and teaching into one concept. But, too often even in these schools, faculties are divided into "performance" teachers and "pedagogy" teachers; course work between the two areas is seldom cross-referenced or coordinated; teaching effectiveness is not scrutinized or tested with the same vigor as performance prowess; and often there remains a feeling of division between the two areas, one which can range from mere estrangement at best to open animosity at worst. Thus a "second best" attitude on the part of many young people toward teaching develops, and they prefer to give their attention to what they perceive as the great, bold adventure of their young careers. And what constitutes this adventure? Entering competitions, playing a concert date here or there, earning a good review, cutting a recording, playing with an orchestra, getting accepted to a certain school or by a special teacher, planning a tour, receiving a grant, studying abroad. These are the primary objectives for most. All of these activities are a valuable part of a young professional's career, to be sure, and it would be folly to curtail any opportunity for achieving as much as possible in these areas.

Rather than incorporating teaching into the adventure, however, musicians often simply regard it as a bread-giving activity, necessary and valuable but about as exciting as a milk cow. For most, the decade of pursuing the glamorous will pass, and after it does, teaching begins then to take on a greater depth, is improved, studied, refined, and often emerges as a powerful force. But why does such a change in attitude take so long? Surely it is in part because seasoned professionals do not emphasize strongly enough, or early enough, the values, challenges, and rewards of teaching.

When will we hear a young professional speak excitedly of his or her own talented student (even if a beginner)? When musicians begin to show how much they value talent at all levels. When will young professionals appear bright-eyed at a pedagogy workshop? Whenever *we* react as much to fine pedagogy workshops as to fine performances. When will young professionals be found scanning new teaching materials at the music store? When *we* start evaluating *all* levels of literature in terms of both musical and pedagogical excellence. When will young professionals discuss heatedly among themselves the relative merits of the various beginning and intermediate methods? When *we* relate musical and technical problems at all levels to what happens as a beginner. When will young professionals become elated over presenting students in recital or in some other form of achievement-evaluation activity? When *we* praise their success as teachers as enthusiastically as we do their success as performers.

Over the years most of us have had to learn how to balance the delicate relationship between our professional activities as performers and as teachers. We have developed that balance individually, oftentimes only after much adjustment. Learning to recognize the importance of both and to define the relationship between the two is a process our students need help with, and they have every right to look to the more experienced for guidance and example. For most students, the teaching component will have to be nourished in the process. As a result, our students will emerge as more sensitive musicians, and the profession may well be rid of a good deal of self-damaging acrimony.

The Teaching Career

In any phase of human endeavor, there exists a large number of worthy individuals for whom nature or circumstance has provided something other than star billing. They come to realize that star billing belongs to a certain type, and that the lights on the top of the tower, although necessary and attractive, do not always represent the best or the most organic segment of that structure.

Many young musicians are astute enough to realize by the time they reach adulthood (often nearing the end of their formal schooling) that they are not destined for star billing, that they have not been given the means — either in terms of talent or time — to attempt a career built on the image of the virtuoso performer. They will elect to continue to perform within their sphere or activity, for groups of peers, for coaches from whom they may continue to seek help and inspiration, and for friends. But they bring themselves to scrutinize the world around them and face squarely the fact that recital performances for the public will not be the mainstay in their careers as musicians and that those performances, when they do occur, will probably be unpaid (or at best paid with only a small honorarium).

This is the point at which the young person may very well ask whether or not it will be possible to earn a living by means of music and, if so, what has to be done to find some measure of financial security. In such a context, institutional security seems attractive initially, so the next goal often becomes that of finding a college or university teaching position. Such a hope is met instantly with a host of negative circumstances. Even in the heyday of the expansion of institutions of higher education, a time of burgeoning numbers of students and little accountability, seeking a position was a process in which stiff competition was to be expected. Only the more brilliant performers, the very aggressive, and the lucky were able to secure such positions, and many worthy applicants were passed over. Recent trends in higher education call for making do with existing resources or cutting back for the foreseeable future. The result is that the odds of being able to land a college teaching job are so poor that the marketplace is teeming with highly qualified young professionals all in heated competition with one another for the few jobs which are advertised and which have managed to escape being cut from the budgets.

The more knowledgeable realize, furthermore, that even securing a college teaching position does not necessarily mean that one has found a secure haven from which to practice one's art. Positions are always subject to budget cuts, even when occupied, and arts programs are often targeted first in difficult times. If the position itself remains stable, a young faculty member always faces the continuing review of contributions both to the institution and the profession. These reviews usually culminate in a tenure decision being made from five to seven years after the job begins. During this process, campus colleagues, some of whom will be from other disciplines, evaluate not only teaching effectiveness, but also the reputation achieved through performance, publishing, conference papers, prestigious invitations or awards, and professional service. Those whose activities, both on and off campus, do not measure up to expected standards will not be offered tenure and will be given notice. Such a process hardly suggests security, as many young faculty members have painfully learned.

Thus with the prospect of obtaining such a post very remote and keeping it somewhat risky, many young professionals are faced with the prospect of having to consider what may be viewed as the last resort before leaving the profession altogether. It is usually expressed in a phrase something like: "Of course one can always teach privately."

It is an unfortunate phenomenon that, in music, pursuing one's profession on an independent basis is often regarded as the last possible and least desirable means of earning a livelihood. Indeed, some prefer to leave music altogether rather than to assume this seemingly modest role.

Certainly private practice is deemed a respectable enough activity in other professions with no hint of second best. Lawyers, doctors, accountants, business consultants, and even spiritual guides — to mention a few — all engage in private practice. Most professions have recognized credentials, such as academic degrees or licenses, and some practitioners offer these as a means of enhancing their following. We know that such credentials tend to instill a sense of confidence on the part of the public, but they are not really a guarantee of excellence. Dull lawyers do appear before the bar and inept physicians do practice medicine. Yet, overall, the professionals of these groups, if judged to some extent initially on credentials, are in the long run successful if they can build a reputation for quality. They are in no way prejudged by whether or not they operate privately, as a member of a consortium, or on the staff of an institution. It should be the same for musicians.

The private teacher too can offer certificates of study, degrees of learning, certification, and membership in professional organizations, many of which require evidence of professional competence. From that point on, success, like that in other professions, should depend upon the ability to build a reputation for quality — no matter what the structure of operation.

In other professions we see frequent patterns of freelance career building. For example, if a young person has completed professional education and has certain services to offer a community (legal, medical, or business services of some kind), a search might be made for some area of the country where those professional services would be in demand. (Such areas can be identified, for example, by studying population density, growth factors, the number of professionals in that area offering such services.) Assuming several such areas might be found, the one selected might be the most attractive for personal reasons. A visit to such an area and talks with professionals there, with chambers of commerce, with church or club groups, might be in order. Once the decision is made the adventure begins. Planning for an initial investment in business space and equipment is in order, as well as a small reserve to keep going for several months while the business takes hold.

Young musicians who do this should realize that young teachers may have to undergo a period of building, during which time there may well be a financial struggle, but then so do young professional men and women in many fields. The market for any service may fluctuate from decade to decade.

Thus they must be prepared to struggle through the lean years, but with the expectation of emerging ten years later as successful, well-established professionals who serve their communities. Difficult and risky? Of course. There will be naysayers, moreover, who believe that no amount of creative effort will result in enough revenues to pay the bills, much less achieve some measure of security. On the other hand, good doctors, dentists, lawyers, CPAs, travel agents, tax consultants, and small business people of all kinds mount successful endeavors all the time, and the current direction in many professions is away from institutional employment, where efforts to achieve efficiency have resulted in wholesale job cuts, toward individual entrepreneurial enterprises.

As far as the music profession itself is concerned, it is time we exercised some self-esteem in the matter of private teaching. We can do this by shifting our focus. We need to forget for awhile that "anyone can hang out a shingle," the negative viewpoint, and remember that some of the greatest teachers in history have at some points in their careers been private teachers. One could begin by pointing out that such was true of Liszt and Leschetizky and go on from there. A firm fix on the positive view of the private teaching profession should blot out the hesitation in answering the question which a young professional might ask, "But after I get my degree in music, what will I do with it?"

Why, build a professional career! Of course, that's what you do with it — and for many that will mean building a career as a professional teacher in the private studio.

Teaching and Mentoring

We have often heard it stated that as music teachers our sphere of influence goes beyond that of providing knowledge about playing an instrument or singing. We have probably reflected at some time on our role in the development of the student as a human being, on the fact that much of our effectiveness as teachers stems from being good psychologists. Perhaps we even have evidence of how our influence has worked favorably in the thinking and development of a young person, as he or she met some point of decision or crisis in life.

Such reflections seem justified, for if one guards against uninvited meddling and is careful to keep in mind that most of us are indeed not trained psychologists, one can often consciously contribute to the quality of a young person's overall lifestyle. Obviously we must believe that music itself is a positive force, and our contribution toward making music a part of a young person's future is in itself a good thing. But over and above this obvious influence, there are many beneficial ways in which we are able to shape a young person's thinking. If we consciously recognize what we can do in this direction, we can possibly become an even more positive force.

The kinds of contributions we might consciously consider are those which will hopefully grow into basic philosophical tenets and determine a person's capacity to deal with life over the years. They will stand as an individual's attributes, whether or not that person becomes a musician. They help determine psychological patterns and reactions to environment. (Lest there be any misunderstanding, these do *not* necessarily have to do with the student's immediate personal problems, such as family relations, school, and dating. Music teachers often find themselves in the position of being asked advice on these specific matters, but how much one is willing to contribute to the solution of these problems is a very complex and highly individual matter. Involvement in these affairs is usually a two-edged sword and should be approached with great caution — not because one doesn't *want* to help, but because one is not usually in a position to know enough to be qualified to offer counsel on delicate personal matters. There is always the possibility that one might end up making things worse by ill-timed or ill-spoken suggestions.)

In consideration of the spheres of influence in which we might act beneficially, we must set our own goals, remembering constantly that what we hope to achieve will always be tempered by the personality of the individual student as well as the impulse deep within most of us to resist new ways of thinking. Let us, however, for the moment consider the following possibilities:

Is it possible to teach the *detail* of a musical composition in such an engaging and creative way that a student can experience a genuine sense of satisfaction in trying to beautify a small thing? Some students will be temperamentally suited to this approach and will take to it easily; but can we challenge ourselves to teach such appreciation to the student whose natural impulse is to broad-brush everything?

Conversely, is it possible to stimulate a student with imagery and energy at a lesson so that he or she is lifted to a plane of consciousness where details which have been worked out synthesize into an intellectual-emotional oneness? Some students will tend to do this by themselves; but can we challenge ourselves to create such an experience for the student whose emotional security seems rooted in moving from one routine task to the next, or even to the one who temperamentally seems to be a plodder?

Is it possible to teach analysis and structure with such enlightened precision that a student learns the efficacy of seeking out symmetry, pattern, order, or logic, and transfers such perception to other aspects of his life? This will be easy for those whose minds tend to operate this way naturally; but the challenge comes in showing such processes to the student whose mind prefers to roam freely.

Conversely, can we impart to every one of our students the

joy of improvisation? Not only to the student who expresses himself easily, but also to the one who regards such spontaneous communication as cruel exposure of a very private world?

Is it possible to teach the joy of listening in such a way as to increase a student's sense of perception in all areas, so that listening not only gets better in areas outside music, but also triggers a sensory process which crosses over to a more acute awareness of what is seen, touched, tasted, or smelled?

Is it possible to guide the student through a performance in such a way that there is born a sense of the delicate balance between careful preparation and adventurous action? Can the student thus learn something about the concept of "calculated risk," a concept which must figure in many of life's decisions?

Is it possible to use music, a nonverbal communication medium, as a means of turning a young person's attention toward man's highest striving for nonverbal communication — the seeking of increased spiritual awareness and understanding? Such a question defies definitive answer, and yet we know that great teaching in any field has at certain rare moments the ability to sensitize the deepest inner consciousness.

Such questions as these only serve as catalysts. Often we will never know if there was any measure of success with a student in these terms. The shy, quiet student will not reverse behavior. The ebullient one will continue to bubble, and the flamboyant one will still swashbuckle. But somewhere, at some point, you may have opened the door to another way of thinking about things; you may have imparted a learning technique which will be brought into play years later; or you may have created a moment of truth that will be carried deeply imbedded in the philosophical armor of your student to be used later in life.

Such far-reaching effects are not so fantastic. How many

of us cherish a comment by an admired teacher — a comment made perhaps even offhandedly — but which for us became a guidepost for the pattern of our lives? Contemplation of such effects brings us face to face with awesome responsibility — but such responsibility is also a source of life-giving challenge.

2

Basic Positions

Performance Attitude

*A*S important as teaching hand position or posture at the instrument is the teaching of certain attitudes about music and music making. These attitudes form a philosophical foundation regarding our art and our relationship to it. For teachers, identifying philosophical issues and formulating a position are very important, for without such a process we often inadvertently buy into opinions or actions in which we really do not believe. These, in turn, can be interpreted by our students as inconsistencies at best or duplicities at worst.

For example, how do we really feel about playing for people, about sharing easily, quietly, and without much self-consciousness the products of our labor? What is our own gut reaction (and how do we influence our students to react) when we encounter that situation in which someone, usually someone who knows little or nothing about music, happily says, "So you're a pianist. Great! Play something!"

This request is perfectly logical. It could reflect a momentary interest on the part of the nonprofessional musician; it could lead to a fan, a concertgoer, or a music consumer. And yet it is the request which most pianists are unprepared to honor most of the time.

Always being prepared to present a sample of one's musical work (under the right circumstances) could be a tremendously potent force in one's personal development and reinforce the position of our art as an important activity in our culture. Yet most traditional pianists are trained from their early student years to play — and to be prepared to play — but once or twice a year. Like a plant or tree, they bloom for a short time and then lapse into months of silence except for practicing and lessons.

This pattern becomes firmly entrenched after several years. By high school age, the student may be studying works of moderate difficulty, but until a given work reaches a state of near completion, it is not secure enough to play in public. By the same token, works studied previously have usually been discarded as soon as they were no longer on the recital or lesson docket. As a result, many students who have studied eight or ten years have no repertoire at all.

The pattern continues right on into young adulthood. Should a young person be pursuing a course of study at a college or university leading to a professional degree in music, a recital may be required as the culmination of the degree work. Here, often for the first time, the student faces the problem of being able to sustain an hour's worth of music. This problem often becomes one of the most difficult aspects of recital preparation, simply because the student has been trained over the years to play constantly but not to maintain a performing repertoire.

What is even more damaging is that without early training in this aspect of the art, the young musician can never hope to achieve that psychological state where playing is a comfortable means of personal expression, a direct line of communication to those who listen. Rather, music making is relegated to a special occasion, attended by nerves and the wish to get through the ordeal somehow. With this kind of conditioning year after year, it is no wonder that the normal excitement attending the act of playing for an audience eventually grows into a grotesque demon for many, riding herd on every performance under the banner of "performance nerves" or "stage fright."

Several habits, established early, could add up to a more healthy pattern. A regular review of repertoire material at lessons should be undertaken — a time-consuming effort, to be sure, but profitable in untold ways. As a first step, teachers might help students make repertoire lists of five or six pieces which have been studied in the past and which are reviewed on a regular schedule for lesson performances at the rate of one piece per lesson, with the cycle being repeated and enlarged continually. Students should come together often to play for each other. (It is my personal belief that these get-togethers can be arranged without reference to present levels of achievement. As pianists we must learn to derive pleasure and inspiration from listening to those who play more beautifully than we do and, by the same token, learn to listen with pleasure and understanding to those who are traveling the roads we have left behind.) At times these informal get-togethers might include visits of guests, such as parent, teachers, and other interested students.

Finally, it would seem that one of the greatest rewards of our art could be the habit of saying to a friend, a loved one, or any human being who you sense might respond: "I would like to play something for you." Translated into philosophical terms, this offer means "I have found something beautiful, and I have invested part of the time I have on this earth to learn how to re-create it. Come, let me share it with you!"

Of course this kind of attitude is filled with pitfalls. Our good-natured audience may request music we don't know or a style we don't play. (Do you play "Deep Purple" or how about a little gospel?) These, once again, are not unreasonable re-quests from the standpoint of the nonprofessional, but such requests often incite embarrassment over the fact that we play only "classical," or we don't have much experience in a larger variety of styles. Often the perfect foil is to be able to do a little bit of music making in some style which is less formal and a little closer to a present-day entertainment format than eighteenth- and nineteenth-century European music. One can learn to improvise a little, or play some Gershwin or even a little boogie-woogie or blues. This icing can often ease the way into a performance of Mozart or Chopin or Debussy, thus demonstrating what one really does play well and selling at the same time. The important thing is to meet an audience and play for it, rather than to cower or back off because of feeling unprepared or uncomfortable with the dynamics of communi-cation.

Yes, one has to be prepared actually to get through a piece. Pianos have to be at least serviceable, and listeners have to devote at least a modicum of attention to the performance (sometimes difficult to command in this age of wall-to-wall canned music). In short, many conditions have to be fulfilled before communication, especially musical communication, can take place. One has to expect an occasional misfire and be prepared to laugh it off as an ill-fated attempt. But learning to roll with the punches is an important part of being a musician. Our art may be our most precious possession, but we have to learn not to let it be represented as simply precious.

The Performance-Career Dream

Knowing as much as we do about the difficulties of our profession, how do we teachers respond to a young pianist who has caught the dream? Should we fan the flame with unrestrained vigor? Should we sound the alarm of caution, having lived long enough to see such starry hopes tempered by the realities of the marketplace? Should we discourage professional aspiration altogether, given the unanswered questions about the future of our art in our cultural hierarchy?

Let us begin to study our position by remembering that the process of attaining adulthood in all aspects of life is to some degree a process of aligning the complexities and reality of adult living with the relatively simple visions of childhood. This alignment may temper the enthusiasm of the child's dream, but hopefully maturity will bring about recognition of new values (in addition to new difficulties) and the envisioning of new goals to replace the simple ones of the child.

The adult perception of reality destroys some childish dreams. Thus not all of us become firemen, undercover agents, or movie stars. By the same token, maturing perception renders other goals increasingly more important, so much so that eventually the taproots of our lives are put down, hopefully strengthened by the very resistance which reality almost always thrusts upon us.

Frequently the first attraction of a youngster to play the piano (and to many other musical activities) comes hand in hand with the concept of being admired — a kind of glamorized stardom. Strong identification is made with great performers, whom audiences cheer, with the never-never land of being a celebrity. Moreover, for the vast majority of the young who are thus enchanted, the promise of a long, rough road to the top — starting today with several hours of hard work — is absolutely no deterrent at all. Quite the contrary, this breed often links hard work and eventual reward psychologically, and the result is a passionate drive for musical self-improvement, often described somewhat romantically as "dedication to the art."

It would be foolish to deny that this drive is needed for musical success, but the drive carries with it an inherent danger. Over a long period of time the expectation of eventual reward becomes very strong, and often that reward remains a solidly frozen concept, the immature one of youth: stardom. Anything less becomes linked with failure at worst or compromise at best. Thus as the adult reality begins to be perceived, as the young adult looks around, an impending feeling of frustration or insecurity begins to hang heavily. Refusing to let go of the original goal, the young person sees the odds against the achievement of this fleeting image grow and grow. It will be hoped, nevertheless, that by a series of lucky breaks, he or she will still somehow make it.

Make what?

It was a childish dream, never properly revised. It was a very necessary and important dream in its place, but at some point a teacher, an experience, or a realization should have contributed the catalyst for enlarging the goal-concept. Even those who do a lot of performing in their careers do not view themselves as the youngster did. And what are the other manifestations of the profession? The collaborative music making, the improvising, the accompanying for dancers, the recording, the entertaining, the arranging, the scholarly research? This work is all work which pianists, as musicians, do as part of their professional life, and many of them work efficiently, happily, without a great sense of frustration or failure. They do so because they were able as maturing adults to face realities, and as a result to expand horizons. They replaced the improbable and the narrow with the new, the unexplored, with a deeper but broader concept of what it means to be a musician.

Thus with proper growth, a young musician should

achieve adulthood in his or her profession with a broad self-image fully developed, so that very real goals may be pursued with confidence and a sense of growing achievement. Such mental well-being is not gained overnight. It needs time to grow, and seeds need to be planted early.

For example, a youngster needs to be rewarded as much for making music with others as for solo performance. Young people who have a flair for using their instruments to entertain (in a light sense) need encouragement which goes beyond mere adult toleration. (Young entertainers usually win quick approval from peers, but adult approval too is valued.) The skills involved in ensemble playing or in entertaining should be taught and stressed. What does it take to develop a first-rate sight reader or a fine improviser? Where is the guidance in exploring the art song literature or that of chamber music? Is there a creative interest in composing?

Too often youngsters arrive at the threshold of young adulthood believing that all of these activities are *extra* pleasures or chores which but attend the mainstream of their activity: learning and performing solo literature. Should we wonder then that they begin to suffer frustration and disappointment — to the point of trauma as they must face the realization that the world of practicing musicians is by and large not made up of those who travel about performing solo before audiences? Should we wonder at the damage to youngsters' self-images as they secretly conclude that in some mysterious way they were "not good enough" to achieve this fantasy?

Yes, it takes time to broaden. It must even steal time from the pursuit of the solo performer's goals. But in the very name of "dedication to the art," it is just this embracing of the art as a whole that is so vital. Our inherited tradition supports this point of view. Make a list of those great pianists of the past who were chamber musicians, who entertained with improvisations on popular tunes, who devoted a major portion of their careers to activities outside public performance (teaching, conducting, or composing), and you will have made a list of the most distinguished musicians in Western music. You can start it with Mozart, Beethoven, Chopin, Liszt. . . .

The Extremely Gifted Student

Sometimes the impact of the gift was evident when the student first auditioned for you. Or perhaps the realization of the student's special talent may have dawned after a few lessons, as potential and rate of growth became apparent. Whatever the mode, the certainty is suddenly lodged in your perception that you are teaching an unusually gifted student, perhaps one of near "prodigy" level, and suddenly your responsibility as a teacher looms in awesome dimensions.

There are many questions teachers must address when they encounter the extraordinary student. Basic to any strategy designed to guide the student is the determination of the extent to which the student as an individual wishes to commit to music. As professional musicians, we tend automatically to assume that the *ability* to achieve the highest levels of musical and technical proficiency is synonymous with the *desire* to do so. Because of our own priorities, it seems incomprehensible that anyone would not want to develop their gifts to the fullest. We learn, however, that such is not always the case, for often such students are good in several areas, and just as often another field of endeavor is chosen over music as the focus of the most intensive effort. The result is a sizeable body of outstanding men and women in many walks of professional life — medical, legal, research, academic, business, to mention a few — who could have been professional musicians if they had so chosen. Indeed, a great number of them continue to make music on a near professional level for most of their lives.

The concept, however, should not be one which causes us to compromise our standard of quality. Rather it leads us to the assurance that the best way to serve the gifted student is to offer the most exacting challenges and the highest level of teaching within us. What may have to be adjusted, rather, is the rate at which we proceed. Sensitivity to this aspect of the student's development means more than simply being able to live with practice time being encroached upon regularly by pursuits of other interests and occasionally being usurped altogether. That part most of us live with rather gracefully. Where we often misstep, however, is in the assignment of repertoire.

Given limited amounts of time with which to work, temptations to shortcut the climb to the highly virtuostic icons of the literature are great. The simple fact that the student has the ability and coordination to scale the difficulties is temptation enough. Often too the student has heard a work, wants to play it, and requests it. If student competitions enter the picture, the display piece is often seen as a vehicle with which to win. Even parental pressure is often strong to indulge in continued use of showy repertoire.

Feeding these appetites moderately is not unto itself a bad thing, but caution must be exercised lest the practice go so far as to court neglect of balanced fare and a wide variety of challenges. One encounters high school students whose ability to toss off several nineteenth-century virtuoso etudes is wondrous, but who have yet to perform a complete Beethoven or Schubert sonata. If Beethoven is thought to be necessary, then it is believed best to skip the early sonatas and learn something like the "Appassionata." If profound musicianship is to be showcased, choose a late one. Mozart and Haydn are deemed less challenging, music which the precocious leave behind in the first few years of study.

This cavalier attitude toward more subtle musical challenges is insidious in that it often results in burnout. Even gifted, facile students grow weary of a steady diet of virtuoso stunts. They often feel they have completed the course, and they do not understand that in reality they have not really addressed themselves to mastering the first lessons. Restructuring their thinking is quite often difficult, because they confuse such work with a "lower" level of achievement.

This is where the rigors of attention to detail, creative thinking, and the mastery of exacting performance can be of particular use. The late Cecile Genhart used the D minor Sinfonia of Bach as a vehicle to teach her students the extent to which exactness of detail and creative demand could be taken. She aimed for and often got "tears of frustration" in lessons devoted to this phase of study.

Once students begin to understand music making in this depth, they can and do set their own standards, creating their own challenges in the process. The supreme difficulty in all music making becomes a reality, and the "easier" literature they wanted to bypass previously now becomes important to them. And of course, as they rise to these new challenges, the beauty of that music takes hold, too, so that they experience both the joy of new discoveries and the vastness of the array of masterworks in the keyboard literature.

If the gifted student does make a strong commitment to music, then the teacher's role becomes one of not only preparing the student for a well-balanced, rounded musical development, but also acting as a mentor in teaching the student to balance the demands of both art and life. There used to be concern about young persons becoming too narrow and naive in their perception of the world around them if they spent too much time focused on their music. That concern is probably not very realistic in view of the extent and speed of communication technology. Young musicians, like all their generation, are in touch with data banks of information, much of which is assimilated in their daily casual contact with the worlds of television, recordings, and computers. Thus the role of the music teacher may no longer need be one which encourages the student to broaden the scope of inquiry. There is, in fact, a pretty good chance that the computer-wise student will be a step or two ahead of the teacher in this regard.

The teacher's role rather becomes the much more complex one of helping the student practice and perfect a process by which underlying values can be identified so that intelligent choices can be made. Every technological breakthrough brings with it a certain excitement, and propelled by a liberal helping of commercial hype, the technology often looms larger and more important for a period of time than it ultimately settles down and becomes. Technological faddism is very seductive when it is in full bloom, and during its time in the spotlight, it can claim inappropriate amounts of time and energy from those who get caught up in the excitement.

Teachers need to be open and informed about the technological world in which their students are living. Having, however, put down roots in aesthetic values and having achieved some degree of success in integrating those values into a lifestyle, teachers must continually help students learn to separate the glitz from the substance. Teacher must point out the ways in which various technological developments support and complement creative, artistic thinking on one hand or, as is often the case, dull and inhibit it on the other. Such identification requires clearheaded thinking, not often easily achieved. Once successfully completed, the teacher will still probably best serve the student by adopting a Socratic rather than a dogmatic approach.

Above all, the gifted student is poorly served by the teacher who cloisters the art, no matter how sincere the impulse to protect and preserve it. Students who persist in being captivated by technology will ultimately regard the old-guard musician as valuable within a limited range, but appreciation and respect for an increasingly isolated tradition may be seriously weakened as its apparent relevance to what is currently happening is eroded. Students who are persuaded to embrace the traditional to the point of excluding lively interest in technology will experience with greater intensity the same painful sensation of fossilization we ourselves know today, combined with the fear that a few decades hence the achievements they work so hard to obtain won't matter much to anyone.

Rather, the teacher and student together must combine their efforts to explore the new, to evaluate it carefully in terms of basic artistic principles, to embrace the useful, and to let pass the faddish. Not that anyone is so omniscient as to be able to determine unerringly which is which. But the process itself will keep the traditions we love in the mix, scrutinize the new carefully, and ensure the continued use of discernment born of sensitivity to aesthetic values. Only in this way can we teach the gifted how to deal with the ever-accelerating changes which are bound to come about in the years ahead.

The Latecomer

Having explored our attitude toward the gifted and the aspiring professional, let us consider how to regard those who seek our help, but who are obviously not well focused on our world of music making, the young or older adults who somehow come from the wrong side of the tracks, musically speaking. This breed often burst into your life with the enthusiasm of a puppy, proclaim being hooked on the muse, and often demonstrate everything known about music (frequently with little or none of the reticence displayed by the traditionally trained piano student).

Typically what you hear is an "original" composition consisting of much repetition of the same harmonic progression, an incessant rhythmic pattern, little dynamic variation, and lots of damper pedal. It is performed with an almost frenetic enthusiasm, showing no physical awareness of the relationship between the performer and the instrument.

Hopefully you swallow your first impulse to tell this poltergeist simply to go away. (Or its nicer version: "You need to find a teacher who can teach you *that* kind of music.") Should you be tempted to answer in this fashion, just remember that this youngster is two steps ahead of you. There is probably already the knowledge that you teach traditional music, but there is also simply the desire to learn more about music in general. Your young enthusiast is apt to tell you that music is the only thing that's important, and that's the reason every aspect of it has to be learned.

This combination of enthusiasm and naïveté is quite often totally disarming. You want to tell this hopeful that you know many eight-year-olds who play the instrument more skillfully, and yet you must ask yourself how strong and how deep is this person's desire to learn about music. You want to point out that technical skills are so far behind that the odds of learning enough to earn a living in music are very slim, and yet you must ask yourself if you have the right to prejudge motives, or set goals, and ultimately assume what role music is to play in the life of this young person.

The fact is that our value code, although it may be born of experience and sophistication, may have very little meaning for this student, and our attempt to dampen the flame of enthusiasm is apt to be construed as a kind of narrowness at best and downright snobbishness at worst. Passing judgments or pronouncing probabilities about the future based on these values are pretty futile activities — at least at this stage.

Headstrong and idealistic, our young student has decided that *success* means finding something (in this case music) to which to relate in a personal way. It does not necessarily mean doing it better than the next guy (competition) or receiving approval for it. Growth means deepening love for this activity (music) and sharing it with others through more direct communication. It does not necessarily imply gaining a reputation as a hot shot performer or getting degrees. Fulfillment means becoming a master. It does not necessarily mean being able to earn a good living with this activity.

"But," we protest, "what will this person be able to do with it?" Meaning, that their proficiency will probably never be good enough to meet the professional standards of the world we know as teachers. Such may be quite true, and assuming it is, there are two possibilities. The first is that you will train a musician who may be headed toward another world of music making, a commercial world driven by a technology which can often bypass traditional skills, with potentially another audience. If you are like most members of the piano-teaching profession, you know very little about that world's professional requirements and chances for success. The second possibility is that as this student matures, music may have to give way to make room for adult responsibility as the need and desire to take on such responsibilities grow. The ultimate solution for many will be compromise. Some will become secretaries or clerks or TV repairpersons or salespersons — and ardent musicians on the side. This state of affairs is not so terrible and not the least bit unusual in or out of music, for countless people in our society regard leisure-time activity as their first love, whether it be golf or chess, writing poetry or breeding dogs, or playing the piano.

Either way, however, we have the tasks of imparting sensitivity to sound, refining enthusiasm with the ability to listen carefully, and teaching how to make choices based on aesthetic values. In the process, let your student live out the youthful dreams and ideals, delaying career advice until the learning experience is much further along, or until such advice is requested. Let us trade our knowledge for enthusiasm. Should this person end up a success in some form of popular or commercial music, a better musician will be the result of studying and your guidance. And should the years ahead produce simply an ardent amateur musician, then this person's life will still have been immeasurably enriched by music. Study may continue, buying concert tickets and collecting recordings may be a way of life, and this music fan will probably make some effort to pass the joy of music on to his or her children. Thus this love affair with the muse is one which is of benefit to all parties.

3

Neglected Rudiments

Inner Hearing

*A*S musicians and teachers, we constantly talk about the necessity of *listening*. We exhort our students to listen to what they are doing: to a melodic inflection, a harmonic change, an inner voice, the balance between the left hand and right hand or, in collaborative music making, the other musicians' parts. In almost all of our urgency, we are sensitizing our students' perception to sound which has been or is being produced. Obviously, such a procedure is well grounded, and its efficacy, as far as it goes, cannot be contested.

Listening, however, in its inception must begin as an inner process, and a powerful inner generation of sound will directly influence both technical security and success in projecting a musical idea. Inner hearing is, however, a private thought process and, like any such mental activity, is carried on without immediate outward signs as to its speed, clarity or strength. If the inner hearing is faulty, the signs which appear are often subjected to various diagnoses, and just as often, the deeply rooted, essentially hidden, inner hearing process is not suspected of being the underlying culprit in technical insecurity, memory loss, or tepid musical projection. As a result, remedies are tried which may help to some degree but which never get to the heart of the problem. Thus, the fault never is completely corrected. Indeed, it won't be until its source has been identified and addressed.

Thought processes which result in inner hearing take place to some degree in all music making, just as conceptual thinking takes place to some degree in all speech. But just as various thought processes result in a wide variety of speaking effectiveness, ranging from incoherent, through scatterbrained, through serviceable, to the articulation of complex abstractions, so too can inner-hearing processes produce music making which ranges from disorganized, through sloppy, through pretty good, to conceptually profound. These inner-hearing processes are referred to with some degree of frequency by good musicians and teachers, but seldom do we give them more than lip service, an occasional dutiful reference to their mysterious ways in a lesson, or our blessing while relegating the hard work of nurturing them to the aural skills classroom.

Yet we are often presented with an array of clues which suggest that our students' inner hearing processes are not very well developed. How many of our students literally will not or cannot sing their piano music lines? They claim they have "no voice." But most practicing instrumentalists and conductors work in rehearsals illustrating their musical ideas all the time in whatever "voice" they can summon up. Something comes out, and whether a rasp or a falsetto, it serves as an extension of what is going on inside. How many students do not respond to aural directions to pick up the music at a certain point in the score? If a teacher asks the student to begin at x and then plays a harmony or a melodic fragment, those students whose inner voice is weak or indistinct will often become hesitant or confused and may have to be given a visual point of departure before they can proceed. How many students hear clearly enough to be able to set a definite, solid tempo in their mind's ear before they begin to play? How many students sit around listening to their inner music making to the point where they become comfortable with the interpretive and emotional content of that music?

Like any skill, inner hearing can be strengthened only by regular attention to its development. Outwardly silent practice every day for a period of time is the beginning exercise. If but little hearing is taking place, attempts to vocalize with occasional promptings at the keyboard to act as a crutch should be undertaken. Like any skill, faulty, intermittent realization will gradually turn into more continuous success if facility is pursued regularly and assiduously. The sticking point is not the actual development of the inner voice. It exists in each of us to some degree, and it will bloom, once it is given the proper nurturing. The problem, rather, is recognizing it as the fountainhead of exciting music making and giving its development the highest possible priority in cases where it is perceived to be weak or faltering. Toward this end, the teacher must explain it, work through exercises for its development at the lessons, be specific in how it is to be practiced each day, and test its progress on a regular basis at the lesson.

Yes, to be sure, such procedures are effort intensive. But without this foundation, clear musical realization, technical security, and artistic independence can never be more than imitative processes, and emerging young musicians will always experience an elusive sense of anxiety in all they pursue, no matter how many hours of hard work attend their efforts. A highly developed sense of inner hearing cannot act as a substitute for the effort of developing all the other necessary skills, but it is the only solid foundation on which to build, and it will grow into an awareness which will become the most valuable musical instrument of all, leading its possessor to an incomparable inner musical life.

Inner Pulse

Having established the inner sound system, the next order of consideration is to give birth to the inner conductor, the conceptual master of the baton. By and large the inner maestro is shortchanged, frustrated in pursuing artistic goals, and generally misunderstood (just as many conductors imagine themselves to be in the professional world).

We are firmly wedded to the idea of counting. We were taught to do it when we were students; we do it with every piece we learn; we teach our students to count; we count for them in our lessons. What then is the advent of this mysterious birth?

The answer lies in the fact that we use counting as a tool with which we learn the rhythm of a piece. Once the rhythm is learned correctly, and in metered music fitted into the general framework of the beat, counting is abandoned and is invoked again only if difficulties in controlling the tempo appear.

The music making then is subjected to the processes through which we garner appropriate stylistic or expressive characteristics. These processes include adding rubatos, shaping of phrases, or broadening cadences. By and large, all this bending usually is done without reference to the basic pulse, but rather with a kind of free-flowing interpretive license, born of knowledge of the style, gleaned from both historical research and experience with performance tradition. With students who are naturally gifted with a strong inner sense of pulse and rhythm, toying with the beat may work just fine, for the result

will be tempered by an overall rhythmic sense which may fluctuate and vary, but which never will become erratic or indulge
in such excess that the rhythmic ideas break down. In students
whose overall rhythmic framework is more fragile, however, the
music making often contracts a discernible lack of vitality,
mixed with inappropriate tempo control, problems of pacing,
and small rhythmic glitches which constantly have to be corrected.

The telltale test of weak underlying rhythmic perception is
the absolute inability to count aloud and play the music. There
is, in short, no conductor, and the result is that technical difficulties dictate tempo change and interpretive license has no
elastic limits.

Conceptually the solution is simple. Learn to play the piece
and count aloud. Since the counting should reflect all interpretive decisions, it should be planned and executed with the skill
of a conductor. A moment's thought should make quite obvious
the fact that the described procedure has nothing to do with the
metronome. (Metronomes can be useful in procedures which
relate to quantifying tempo and sometimes controlling tempo,
but hours of practice with the machine ticking away will not
give birth to the inner maestro, and without that even tempo
control often remains stubbornly unreliable in any performance
situation where the adrenalin is flowing.)

Learning to play and respond to your own flexible beat is
easier said than done. Often the technical coordination of the
piece breaks down completely with the interjection of the beat,
no matter how free. Oftentimes learning the process leads to
feeling ridiculous because one can't get the sequence of numbers to flow properly. Oftentimes one counts irregularly, following the rhythmic pattern rather than the pulse. In short, the
piece must frequently undergo an overhaul period wherein it
has to be relearned to a substantial degree.

Once the playing has been retooled, however, the benefits

are almost always spectacularly apparent. Even in the process of changing the relationship between the rhythmic patterns and the pulse framework, the shaping of the pulse itself and the resulting rhetoric of the rhythmic flow become rejuvenated expressive forces. One becomes very much aware of the fact that a newly generated power is revitalizing the music.

Once this procedure is in place as a regular part of daily practice, the ability to act as your own conductor will grow, often rather quickly. As it does, it imparts not only the expected rhythmic vitality to the music making, but also a new sense of technical command, a bonus benefit which to some may be surprising. The refocusing of attention on the force driving the music forward tends to subdue some part of the conscious effort linked with the technique during earlier learning stages. As a result, the technical process discards an inhibiting factor which is no longer needed and flows more easily. This forward motion and its resulting technical benefits can often be felt so clearly that it seems like one has undergone some kind of miracle cure for one's technical ailments. Not so. Such liberation is not a substitute for careful technical preparation, but it can aid enormously in polishing a piece once the solid preparation has been set in place.

Adele Marcus would often say to a young pianist after an impressive performance of a difficult or complex work: "You must learn to count, my dear," and of course she was not referring to rhythmic incorrectness, but rather to an unoccupied inner podium. Indeed, it behooves us all, at some point, to "learn to count."

Harmonic Consciousness

Most eighteenth- and nineteenth-century keyboard literature is built on the harmonic system we learn to recognize and label in traditional theory classes. That system can become very complex on occasion, but most of the time its use tends to center around a central core of well-known chords and progressions, which composers ingeniously use and reuse in a wide variety of ways. Moreover, the harmonic system has evolved expected patterns of stress and inflection, the patterns often changing from period to period and undergoing surprising or unexpected deviation in the hands of master composers.

The extent to which performers strengthen their awareness of this aspect of the music is often an indication of their deftness in handling both technical and interpretive values. There is a residual level of harmonic consciousness in all of us. Most of us "analyze" the music at some point in our own study or, if teaching, point out the harmonic scheme to our students. If such an analysis is regarded as essentially irrelevant to the music, it recedes to a level where it remains unhelpful, by and large. If, on the other hand, such knowledge becomes interwoven as an integral part of the process of aural recall, it becomes an important part of a support system which undergirds and strengthens both technical execution and expressive clarity.

Just where the appropriate level of harmonic consciousness lies is difficult to determine and may differ with each individual. Surely it is possible to place too much focus on the continuing processing of information which might indeed be regarded as compositional mechanics. Visions of the magic of Schubert sonatas being reduced to a series of Roman numerals are horrifying to the sensitive, as well they should be. On the other hand, the key change up a minor third or the tension implied in the augmented sixth chord is a part of that magic, if not its totality, and recognizing and responding appropriately to that knowledge can often open up the way to the perception of more sublime mysteries.

Harmonic consciousness and its use might be compared with spelling. In order to write effectively, you do not have to be a good speller. But sensitivity to words, their meaning, their sound, and their use will probably lead to the kind of continued study which will result in being a very competent speller. Furthermore, writing effectively requires that some level of the mental process be engaged in using words fluently with an attending flow of serviceable spelling.

Students often regard a teacher's testing of the level of harmonic consciousness as a curious exercise. A teacher's request for the identification of the key center in a development section or the name of a particularly colorful altered chord is often greeted with a kind of unspoken surprise that the hard work of arriving at a meaningful interpretation of a masterpiece would be interrupted by a theory quiz. It is precisely at this point that we as teachers must try to describe the subtle underlying relevance.

Strengthening harmonic consciousness often results in one of the slowest growth patterns in traditional piano study. The study of reading procedures or improvisational skills will undoubtedly help, but these skills are often accorded an ancillary niche in the overall study program, if included at all. Formal analysis is also a step in the right direction, but the information gleaned from the activity must cross over at some subliminal level into the mental process which drives the performance.

Reexamining the role of the harmonic framework and aligning it with expressive points of tension and release, not once but many times as an interpretive exercise, causes the harmonic consciousness to grow. In addition, learning to reduce the music to its underlying harmonic components is a valuable phase of study which should be carefully cultivated. The process must take into account the main harmonic framework of the music as well as all the decorations. One begins to sense what is, indeed, the fundamental harmonic drive and how that is altered, enhanced, delayed, or shaped by the inventiveness of the composer in dealing with nonharmonic elements. Dissonance and consonance become forces which react on one another in more meaningful ways.

Such exercise leads to a mastery of harmonic inflection which is as subtle and sensitive as the use of words in language. Such exercise also ultimately results in deep understanding of one of the fundamental dimensions of almost all keyboard music and the understanding, in turn, leads to security and authority in its projection.

4

Neglected Skills

Sight Reading

E NOUGH has been written about the matter of sight reading for piano students to fill several volumes. We are all aware of the travesty of keyboard players who play difficult literature — carefully prepared — extremely well but who falter embarrassingly when asked to read a simple accompaniment. We are all committed to imposing a regime on such students to be sure they bring their reading skills up to snuff. At the risk, however, of frustrating efforts to correct an admittedly deplorable state of affairs, perhaps a few words should be voiced in defense of those for whom reading is a problem.

As with other skills, reading is dependent on a basic aptitude for the process. We tend to regard those who read poorly as simply the product of laziness or willful disregard of the process. And yet the fact remains that there are some good students, even musically gifted students, for whom the process of reading is difficult, even to the point of being alien to the natural bent of their mental processes.

These students are often gifted in other ways. They may possess good analytical powers and very likely memorize easily. They are often well coordinated physically once the mental imagery to trigger neuromuscular response has had a chance to set in. And indeed, because they work best after the music is conceptually transferred from the written page to some other equivalent set of images, they often are very secure within those equivalents even under pressure; they thus are often dependable performers when operating on their own terms.

(It is tempting in this context to point to the fact that those who are extremely gifted readers often tend to be impatient with detailed work, frequently do not take easily to the mental processes which internalize the music, and sometimes are very insecure in any performance situation in which the score is not a part. Such observations are rife with exceptions and tend not to extend the full measure of appreciation for the reading gift. The bottom line, of course, is quite simply that different aptitudes are given to different individuals.)

Incorporating sight reading as a regular part of instruction at the beginning levels will go a long way toward strengthening reading skills for all students, whether highly gifted in this direction or not. Such happy circumstances, however, are not always the case, and as teachers we often encounter students who do not read well. Some of these students do not have much aptitude for the process and have been allowed to grow well beyond beginning stages by working around this deficiency. Thus, as teachers we need to extend the same patience and understanding to those who do not have an aptitude for reading as we do to students for whom other areas of music study are difficult. Before we all nod our heads in wise approval of what seems an apparent platitude, let me interject a few personal observations from the point of view of someone who did not have the benefit of being guided into good reading habits as a beginner and who fell prey to many frequently encountered suggestions intended to correct reading deficiencies.

Those who are poor readers are told to go read every day and improvement will be forthcoming. Not so. Attempting to read every day can be a frustrating experience which only serves to underscore for the ungifted practitioner the agony of wrongly perceived rhythms and notes.

"Read collaboratively," the poor are told, so you are forced to keep going in spite of your errors. "Keeping going" often leads to total disorientation after a few upsets with stopping as the only possible course of action. At this point one can add embarrassment in front of peers to the list of reading deterrents. We are told never to look at the keyboard in order to ensure constant contact with the flow of the music as it is read, but for keyboard players whose sense of spatial perception is tied up with visual oversight, this can spell discomfort and tension.

Persistent attempts to apply all of these regimes result in a kind of reading survival mentality. It often leads to the facility to read more difficult literature atrociously; to keep going by admitting a degree of sloppiness which is often totally foreign to temperament and training as a musician. Persistence in this exercise may result in a psychological revulsion for the entire process nurtured by continued embarrassment and futility.

In short, these cure-alls did not work for me. A turning point finally came when I sought ways to prevent those of my students who were nonreaders from falling into the same uncomfortable patterns I had experienced for years. I asked questions of myself, and the answers led to a solution, at least for me.

By nature I recoil from the haphazardness imposed by my lack of reading aptitude; then, I reasoned, I must find a reading situation in which I am comfortable while controlling all elements: keyboard positions, rhythmic flow, up-to-tempo playing, all the notes in place, eye comfortably on the score. I answered myself by realizing that, in order to fill that bill, I'd have to go back to a *beginning level.* Well then, I rejoined in my inner dialogue, do so.

I spent a summer reading through the beginning materials from all available methods and composers. I learned a large amount of literature, and for the first time I had fun reading. From beginners' books, I advanced to level 1 for several weeks and read through the gamut of available literature. Level 2 came next, and so forth.

I learned thus to read as I had learned to play the instrument in the first place. But this time, with technique to play the material obviously not a factor to claim my attention, I was able to fill in the skills I needed to become a good reader, skills not as natural to me as some but ones which I developed. I was a good sight reader — of very easy material, to be sure — but the music making was neither substandard nor did it admit undo lack of control in the name of reading facility. I could keep my self-respect as a musician and as a consequence enjoyed the process.

Since that summer, I have used this procedure with good results with students who did not read well. No, the end of this true confession is not that my students and I became crackerjack readers, able to tackle the most formidable challenges with aplomb. Those challenges remain the domain of those whose aptitude for reading is strong, who received early guidance in the process, and who were able to develop their talent to a wonderful, useful art. However, like many musicians, my students and I have developed into quite serviceable readers after much careful, hard work within carefully chosen parameters. We will continue to improve.

Collaboration

Part of the reason that collaborative music making for pianists is relegated to the role of second-class citizenry lies in the fact that the collaborative literature, much of which ranks high among the most glorious expressions in Western music, is not heard by students with the same frequency as the solo literature. Consider the number of performances a student might come across in his early years of a famous Beethoven sonata, say, for example, the "Appassionata." The work might be under study by peers, heard at competitions, performed by famous artists on piano recitals. Soon the work becomes familiar enough so that the student is motivated to want to learn it, to make it a part of his repertoire. Consider the number of performances the same student might come across of the "Archduke" Trio, an equally famous work in its own genre. The answer is obvious, and so is the resultant motivation to learn the piece.

If we are thus to inspire our students to want collaborative experiences, we are going to have to arrange for such performance to become more integrated into the fabric of students' activities. How often do we invite a guest artist instrumentalist or singer to our piano student recitals to present appropriate literature with the participation of our students? How many competitions on the student level are geared to collaborative participation, as opposed to quick fix accompanying in which the pianist's contribution is never adjudicated? How many chamber music rehearsals have taken place in our studios over the past year? How many lessons have been devoted to the problems presented by the piano score of a collaborative musical project? In short, until we as teachers change our day-to-day actions with regard to collaborative music making, we cannot expect our student's attitudes to change, or their development to end up in a profile vastly different from the one we deplore in this regard.

Another aspect of our students' reluctance to get involved in collaborative music making lies in the way in which the pianist's best efforts are often regarded by both his peers and our colleagues. As a preface to the pursuit of this complaint, let it be recognized that indeed not all music making in which the pianist is called upon to participate is, in fact, collaborative, assuming some semblance of equal or near-equal contribution is implied by the term. Obviously, some piano parts are clearly accompanimental. Some of those are orchestral reductions, and although they can be awkward and demanding technically, they tend often to be regarded as being there only to support a featured solo part. Some song accompaniments offer but relatively simple homophonic support for the singer.

Even so, the pianist who participates is often regarded by both the other musicians and the coach as a service tool whose task it is to perform in whatever way it is so directed. In most such circumstances, the pianist is never asked to initiate a musical idea and often is not consulted in matters of tempo, phrase shaping, dynamic levels, retards, or balance. The pianist is told when to "play out" and when to let others shine. Most veteran chamber musicians and vocal coaches act as if the pianist never had a creative thought, and, if one is ventured, the underlying assumption is that the literature under consideration is, after all, not the pianist's literature, and the "veteran" of the collaborative literature knows best in the last analysis. This even extends often to the technical feasibility of many problems wherein pianists are asked to accord latitude to instrumentals or singers in order to facilitate execution, but the converse is almost never granted, pianistic difficulties being rather regarded as a result of a shortage of technique, talent, or practice time.

Collaborative music traditions tend to exclude the pianist from the leadership role in determining the overall concept or the musical effect. Notable exceptions exist. A vocal coach or accompanist by definition has a strong hand in shaping the basic musical content of a performance. On occasion, in academic settings, it is the pianist who is meeting a recital requirement and who by virtue of the parameters of the exercise must act as the musical guide for the performance. But unless those ground rules are in place, the keyboard player is ordinarily the last choice as the musical director of the collaboration.

All of these circumstances lead to experiences for the student pianist which are less than enjoyable and sometimes downright demeaning. Conversely, most pianists do not approach collaborative music making with a superior attitude by any means. It would be indeed a pleasure, therefore, for them to be regarded more often as a true collaborator rather than as an obedient accompanist, certainly in the literature which suggests true collaboration and to at least an appropriate extent in literature more oriented toward the soloist. We as teachers and musicians need to support collaboration to the fullest and sell it to our students, for the rewards in terms of music making can be without equal. We also need to take steps to ensure that the *collaboration* experience is, indeed, just that.

Improvisation

The art of improvisation is a rather extraordinary aspect of keyboard playing which has in past eras been deemed an integral part of being a musician, but which today has all but disappeared from the scene in the experience of many pianists. The first music written *per se* for a keyboard instrument was in all probability music improvised before worship services and later notated. In the great competitions of the past, on various occasions demanded by nobility of famous musicians, an integral part of testing musicianship was to test the ability to improvise. In all probability, Mozart improvised his first six sonatas and played them in public before he wrote them down. The great virtuosi of the mid-nineteenth century dazzled and delighted their audiences with improvisations on popular airs of the day. Thus improvisation as a practice flourished from the beginning of keyboard music right up to the end of the nineteenth century.

What happened?

Shortly after the twentieth century dawned, it was as if a plague had swept across the profession and had killed all species of improvisation insofar as its continuing tradition was concerned. A new breed of pianist emerged, one who was devoted to studying the past for stylistic correctness, who developed a fine technical prowess, who played a large repertoire, who explored little-known music of the past, who even cautiously played some music of his own time, but who by and large showed no inclination toward revitalizing improvisation.

Curiously enough, a new, wild shoot of the old art sprang up with the birth of a new kind of music. It was reborn in New Orleans at the turn of the century, part and parcel of early Dixieland. It grew through four decades under the generalized heading of jazz. And although for the past couple of decades it has been partially supplanted by notation and altered by technology, it remains at the heart of that movement.

But improvisation at the piano continues to languish outside the field of jazz. If one speculates about the reason for this sudden demise, one is struck by the fact that improvisation vanished at that point in history when composers were not necessarily expected to be highly skilled performers; and vice versa, good performers were not very often composers. Yet this twofold identity is vital to improvisation, for, after all, to improvise is a creative process, one in which performance and creation take place simultaneously.

One might point to the fact that the various means of composition employed in the twentieth century have become too complex to lend themselves easily to improvisation. Such a suggestion is, however, suspect, if for no other reason than that great jazz pianists have been using many of those complex compositional techniques during the past decades — in a less concentrated form perhaps than in written music, but then such is the nature of improvisation. Moreover, although technical means may be basic, most composers still feel that the musical idea is important, and improvisation, an art based on an active ear in playing, conceivably could conceive the idea first and let the means follow.

The reasons for the disappearance of improvisation are of more than academic interest, because they may be the same reasons underlying a breakdown of communication between the composer and the performer. Improvisation was traditionally in the style of the day and often was the workshop that composers used not only to refine their own ideas (which they subsequently distilled and wrote down), but also to keep their audiences up to date with (and to some extent conditioned to) their newest thinking. It seemed reasonable to assume that the Viennese audiences who heard Beethoven improvise regularly at musical soirees had a good chance of being the first to take in their stride the "newness" of the written-down works.

Having observed the historical role of improvisation as well as its function as a catalyst for the dissemination of contemporary music, it would seem wise for us to begin trying to pick up the pieces of this aspect of piano playing and see if we can reestablish its importance as a necessary skill for the pianist. Its nonexistent state can be easily observed in that so few professional pianists improvise fluently (outside the field of jazz), and traditionally trained student pianists are almost always petrified at the thought of sitting down and "making up" something.

Where do we start? Well, excellent materials do exist: books of instructions and exercises which try to prime the pump, both in traditional styles and jazz styles. These can be useful, but in addition we must eventually somehow free the concept of improvisation from the confines of exercises, assignments, and regimen. Along with the skills presented by the materials, there have to be "messing around" times: discovering a sound ("don't know what it is, but it sure turns me on"), banging out an infectious rhythm, tossing a figuration — a musical gesture—back and forth between the hands (or better still, between two players). In short, having unrestricted fun at the instrument.

Skilled pianists who decide to improvise are always put off at how poor they sound. Their musical ideas sound trite; the flow is impossible to maintain; and their ears tell them they have miles to go before they even begin to sound as good as a run-of-the-mill cocktail pianist, stylistic differences aside. This ineptness results in being completely turned off with the idea of developing an improvisatory technique.

Several things should be remembered, however. Improvisation begins with an idea, and each idea has its parameters. Learn to stick with one short idea, changing first one parameter a little, then focus on the next. Do not try to change more than one thing at a time in the beginning stages. If a five-note motive has a given melodic pattern, change it but leave the rhythm and harmony intact. Then change the rhythm using the same melodic lines and harmonic underpinning. Then reharmonize the version with which you are most familiar and comfortable. Later, after you have exhausted all possibilities which come easily to mind, one at a time, try to change more than one parameter simultaneously.

If you become bored with melodies which emphasize only the pitches of the supporting harmonies, try constructing appoggiaturas or placing sharper dissonances at harmonic strong points. Remember what works well and what does not. If you become bored with rhythmic patterns which seem mundane, work with syncopation. If your initial harmonic creativity seems rooted in tonics, subdominants, and dominants, try to modulate, or use an altered chord, or add sevenths, ninths, or thirteenths to the harmony. See what polytriads please you and what ones don't.

"But," you protest, "this isn't really improvisation. This is just combining variation with theoretical elements which are quite traditional and which have all kinds of restrictions." The answer is, of course, that the art of improvisation is nothing more than on-the-spot variation of patterns and materials which are already well known to the improvisor, and no matter how free or inspired the momentary flight may appear, there is always a basic set of guidelines at work. The impression of freedom results when the improvised deviation from these guidelines becomes so deft that illusion results. Magicians deal in such deftness and illusion, and their magic, too, is born of discipline and practice.

So resist the discouragement born of initial ineptness. It is like learning to ride a bicycle. You can't have fun on it until you learn to balance it, and to learn to balance it you have to be willing and brave enough to fall down a few times, knowing that the chances are against irreparable damage resulting from the tumbles. Yes, the wobbly stage must be endured and conquered. But after that, just look at the roads ahead and what adventure they promise!

Part II

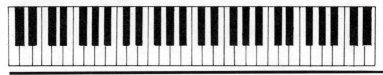

Virtuoso Studies

5

Extension Exercises

Scheduling Practice Time

MOST of us have given nods of approval at one time or another to the old saying, "actions speak louder than words," and certainly we can think of a multitude of ways in which the saying is applicable to our students' working habits. We expect good students to show us with their attitudes, and to some extent in their lifestyles, just how music and working in music rate. Promises count for little, and good intentions only prove to be a source of irritation if they are rarely supported by solid efforts.

But what if suddenly our perspective were altered and we became the student who scrutinized the teacher's lifestyle vis à vis musical goals. Would the teacher's model turn out to be exemplary? Most of us would admit to imperfection quite quickly.

Most of us quickly argue that time is the one factor which

prevents us from working at the keyboard as much as we feel
we ought. There are, after all, commitments to teaching, to
family, to managing a home or a yard, to other employment
perhaps, to social or civic duties — the list could be endless. And
yet we must somehow fight our way through this maze of adult
responsibilities to reserve some time for study, growth, practice,
and even reflection, if we are to realize our own musical potential. If we do not, we fail not only ourselves but our students as
well.

We must remember that the world of the child, the teen-
ager, or the young adult is just as crowded and complex as ours.
It is easy to make the mistake of viewing that world in simplistic
terms because, by our adult standards, consequences of action
or nonaction seem less far-reaching. But stop and reminisce a
little, and you will realize that the responsibilities of school are
just as great from the student's viewpoint as are the responsibilities of job (earning a living or homemaking) from the
adult's. And social pressures are felt perhaps even more keenly
by the young, inasmuch as they are still learning how to fit into
the world of their peers and have the adult world to deal with at
the same time.

Once the complexity of our students' lives is realized, we
begin to see that, if we as teachers cannot find time to work in
our art, if we cannot somehow lead a busy life and still get to the
piano, then we have not solved a problem in our own lives
which we expect our students to solve in theirs. Furthermore
we provide a painfully good example of someone who ostensi-
bly represents the concept of integrating music making as a part
of one's lifestyle but who somehow doesn't manage to get it
done in actuality.

Now this may seem like pretty harsh judgment. After all,
one manages to get through what seems like the necessary
duties of a day and ends up with maybe forty-five minutes of
free time sometime after supper, coupled with a sense of ex-

siderably. Third, the *sostenuto* pedal is one of the least stable mechanical devices of the modern-day piano. Even on well-maintained, fine instruments notes often "hang up," thus continuing to sustain right along with the sound which was originally "set" by the pedal. Often the reverse effect takes place, so that one or more of the notes in the "set" sonority are lost too quickly as the ensuing passage is played. These uncertainties make it desirable to have planned and practiced a backup pedaling which uses only the damper pedal in case mechanical trouble develops at the last moment before or during a performance.

One other reflection might be in order before rushing to solve a pedaling problem with the use of the *sostenuto* pedal. If the *sostenuto* pedal is not specifically indicated by the composer, it is likely that the composer was attempting to create a sonority with the use of the damper pedal in conjunction with careful voicing, balance, and perhaps some measure of half-pedaling or damping. The sonority hoped for will be one which is quite different from one created with the use of the *sostenuto* pedal. One may ultimately opt for the one which makes use of the *sostenuto* pedal as the most satisfactory solution. On the other hand, one may find the parameters the composer used, sensitively controlled, to produce a more appropriate and more attractive sound. At least one should experiment without the quick fix of the *sostenuto* pedal, not only to explore the sound concept composers might have imagined, but also to develop more sophisticated damper pedaling techniques which can be called into service when needed.

The Una Corda *Pedal*

Advice on the use of the *una corda* pedal can differ widely from teacher to teacher. At one end of the spectrum are those who eschew its use with the admonition that one is apt never to learn

The Sostenuto *Pedal*

Most teachers and pianists are almost immediately fascinated by the sound potential of the *sostenuto* pedal, in the middle position of pianos with three pedals. The idea of being able to sustain sounds, "set" them with the pedal, and then play around their continuing sonority with a variety of other textures and touch forms is an exciting concept in itself, and it seemingly offers modern-day solutions to the realization of problematic pedal points in much late-nineteenth and twentieth-century music.

Although the device was invented near the end of the nineteenth century, it was not in common use on pianos until the second or third decade of the twentieth century, first on pianos manufactured in the United States, and then, after the middle of the century, on European grands. Composers did not begin to call specifically for the special effects associated with the use of the *sostenuto* pedal until close to 1950, and when such use was called for, it was usually quite clearly indicated in special directions. Thus using the *sostenuto* as a device with which to address knotty problems associated with the use of the damper pedal is an option open to us, but such a procedure has its own set of pitfalls which should be considered in the process.

First of all, the *sostenuto* pedal takes time to "set." In the context of rapidly moving passage-work, an unwelcome break in the flow, the meter, or the texture may be a stumbling block to getting a clean fix on the sonority which it is desirable to sustain. Second, if one does get a good fix, the notes of the sustained sonority may be reactivated by playing those notes of the subsequent passage which are strong partials in the over-tone series of the sustained notes. The resulting effect may be one in which these notes ring out far more resonantly than their neighbors. This may be perceived as uneven tone production in the passage-work, thus marring its beauty or effectiveness con-

haustion which makes you realize you're not as young as you used to be. This realization is quickly followed by the conviction that even if you forced your way to the piano, you would be too tired to get any real work done anyhow. Quite true, but maybe this is the moment to sit down and rethink your living patterns and search for some answers.

These answers must be arrived at on an individual basis, of course, and what will work for one person won't necessarily work for the next. But we can take comfort in the fact that most of us reach this point at some time or another and that we are thus not alone. Even those who seem to be regular in their own work find that life gangs up on them at times, and dry spells result.

Some questions can be asked at this point that might serve as catalysts for restarting the motor. One of the things which helps many musicians to get started is to begin thinking about music itself: the piece you always wanted to learn, or one put aside half finished, or a technical routine to put you back in shape, or the pleasure of getting to some chamber music a friend once suggested you work on together, or sight reading some teaching materials you do not feel at home with yet, or improvising on the chord progression you teach in order to illustrate more fluently what might be done with this material.

Whatever sparks your interest will, for many, rejuvenate your energy as well, even in the late hours of the day. For others, once an interest is achieved, a rescheduling process may have to take place. If late evening is not your time to be alert, then see if you can choose some more routine task for that hour — a task you usually get done earlier in the day, but which doesn't require as much concentration as music making does. Some astute shifting could give you an earlier block of free time for the music.

If such rescheduling doesn't work, then you may be forced to the task of having to make a choice or two in your life. Most of us have had the experience as teachers of pointing out the seemingly merciless facts that one cannot do everything, and that where music is concerned, considerable cutting back of other activities has to take place sometimes in order to make the kind of time necessary for progress in this demanding art. We point this out, indeed, to both students and parents on occasion. Yet we somehow woo ourselves temporarily into thinking we can escape the consequences of these facts.

If choices have to be made, then only you can make them. If indeed your life is so structured as a result of other responsibilities that you can find no time to continue to grow as a musician, then so be it. At least facing that situation squarely will clear the air, and whatever frustration results from not being able to work will simply have to be endured with the hope that the future will grant a change for the better. (People in hospitals, military service, or other confining environments have had to endure such periods.)

On the other hand, if merely the pace of life or the lure of fashionable living has seduced you into participating in many activities which basically are not as valuable to you as music making, then indeed choices not only can be made — they *need* to be made, and as quickly as possible. Only you can be the judge.

And if you are successful in finding a little time to work, do not, above all, listen to the voice of futility. If the voice whispers that you won't be able to sustain your newfound efforts, then answer it by realizing that all work schedules are maintained by constant renewal. It is not so much a matter of falling off, for we all do that. The trick is to pick yourself up and begin again — time and time again. If you do this, over the long run, you will find that indeed you do have a creative life of music making; progress will be made; goals will be achieved. And as teachers, we will be solving firsthand the problem of keeping music making an active part of our own lives. In turn, these actions will speak louder to our students than our words.

Strengthening Weak Areas

The more experienced we become as teachers and musicians, the more we tend to perfect our area of expertise. We refine whatever it is we already do well; we pursue in depth the specialties that over the years have become identified with our work; we rightfully assume an attitude of authority when dealing with our thing.

The efficacy of all of this is not to be questioned. Whether we consider ourselves superb teachers, or performers of a certain segment of the literature (such as Bach or Schubert or French impressionism) or of a certain type of activity (such as the teaching of beginners or developing gifted high school level students or performing chamber music), most of us know where our strong points lie, where our interest burns most brightly, and certainly we are well advised to make the most of our attributes.

There is, however, one aspect of our own development which is apt to be neglected when such emphasis goes on for years. Such an aspect has its roots in the kind of experience we may not have encountered since our own student days. It is born of the learning experience in which enough resistance is encountered to make one somewhat uncomfortable.

We see this principle in operation all around us, and we realize that *degree* is of critical importance in its effectiveness. We cut back our plants in order to shape them and to stimulate them to more luxuriant growth, but if we go too far we can damage them. We use physical exercise to build muscular prowess, mildly traumatizing our tissues so that they will renew themselves with greater strength. If we go too far or too fast, we can cause physical damage.

To bring this principle closer to our field, ask yourself if when you were a student you ever lived through a period of time, took a series of music lessons, or a course during which you were very uncomfortable or moderately insecure or mildly traumatized — but also during which time you learned an enormous amount or developed faster than ever or gained a new level of discipline which was heretofore unknown to you. Later, from a vantage point of more maturity, you admit to yourself that although you went through hell at the time, the benefits to you in the long run far outweigh the discomfort.

In this context, let us remind ourselves that a considerable number of extremely effective teachers have gained reputations of being not merely "demanding" but downright unpleasant with students who do not please them, thus creating scenes which disturb the student. Some teachers believe sincerely, in fact, that they must place extreme demands on a student, pressuring that student until the psychological point is reached at which singleness of purpose emerges, the only desire being to learn, to embrace self-discipline, and to please the teacher. (Such a procedure is in fact widely accepted in other kinds of learning situations, particularly those involving "new" students: plebes in military academies, pledges in fraternal orders, novices in religious orders, rookies on teams, even freshmen in some colleges.)

How much one may adopt such a method as a teacher depends upon several factors: one's basic philosophical premises, the age level of the students one deals with, the inherent motivation and goals of the students, the sensitivity of a given student, and last but hardly least, one's own predilection for applying necessary pressure. Should one incorporate this technique as a part of teaching, one must be prepared to regard it as a high-voltage procedure, extremely effective with proper use, but also somewhat dangerous.

The point of this discussion, however, is not to examine the advisability of using such a tool in teaching so much as to ask oneself whether after years of comfortable professional activity, personal encounter with an area of relative insecurity would produce a valuable learning experience and result in a period of rapid growth. Probably it would, if we can muster the effort and stand the strain.

What would constitute such an experience? Well, obviously the answer depends on the person. For some, the simple matter of performing in one's own student recital would do the trick. Or perhaps asking for critical comment on either your teaching or your performing from someone whose authority you respect. For others, tackling areas of your development that are weak and have always made you uncomfortable might be in order. If your sight reading is poor, create a situation in which you *have* to sight read. If your ear was never really great, find an ear-training class in which your bête noire will be exposed. If you don't improvise, join a group where under guidance you have to improvise for others, and they for you. Yes, it may mean baring your impoverished creative impulse before the scrutiny of others, but it also may force you to begin thinking musically in totally new ways. Does one particular period of music make you feel uncomfortable? Learn music from that era and play it for friends. Do you not memorize easily? Make a special study of the subject and perform by memory regularly.

This list of activities can be created only by you, for you must determine your own needs. The point is that in planning your professional activity, dig around for those areas in which you know you are not comfortable. And, within reason, put some pressure on your tender spots — even if this makes you feel temporarily inadequate, insecure, and exposed. Not only will you be apt to stimulate your own growth beyond the usual measure, but also you will refresh your own experience with regard to the frustration that sometimes attends learning. This fresh experience will in turn give you renewed understanding for the bumps and knocks some of your own students are going through. For we *do* forget how it feels as a result of years of comfortable professional activity, and literally putting ourselves in a vulnerable position for a time can result in a valuable psychological sharing with our students' efforts, each at his own level.

Taking Stock

One of the most difficult tasks a teacher faces is that of periodic stocktaking. Most of us feel the need once every so often to try to stand back from our work as a teacher in order to obtain some kind of overview. Hopefully, out of such a process will come some soul-searching and some improvements.

Since teaching is an activity which involves our total being, such an overhaul becomes extremely difficult. If we become too aware, we end up with only self-consciousness. If we become too self-critical, we short-circuit inspiration. And yet without any attempt at self-evaluation, we may well deprive ourselves of one of the most potent stimulants for growth. In order for this process to work properly, we need to develop techniques of perception which are somewhat indirect. We need to sharpen our intuitive sense about our own method of operation without bringing it to a halt under the full glare of critical light.

Sometimes reflections about one's own teachers, both our favorite and our not-so-favorite ones, can help us to identify basic characteristics, both good and bad, and can cause us to ask ourselves how much these characteristics are evident in our own teaching.

Reflect, for example, and ask yourself what were the two or three most inspiring lessons you ever had. Then go on and see if you can identify *why* they were so inspiring. At this point it might be easy to attribute such inspiration to the force of the personality of the teacher who gave you that lesson. But don't simply stop there, for if you can think hard enough to identify a few of the abstract qualities which made that lesson inspiring, you may have given yourself a goal toward which to strive.

What were the two or three most powerful lessons you ever had? To be inspired is one thing. To be changed as a result of contact with enormous power is quite another. It is possible that such contact produced mild trauma rather than inspiration, and yet the result was a personal change which took you down a new road and which you remember as a significant turning point. Such profound changes come about partly because of a teacher's qualities, but also partly because the student is ready for them. At this point we can ask ourselves how often we take the time to try to sense how and when our own students are ready for an experience of this type.

Do you remember teachers who were good teachers, but who had mannerisms that drew attention away from the subject matter at hand? And do you remember how students oftentimes mimic these mannerisms, cruelly perhaps, but tellingly? None of us teachers can escape mannerisms, but perhaps we can try to catch ourselves using too often our favorite phrases, teaching too often a pattern of predetermined steps, responding to our students' playing too often with the same criticisms.

We must remember that the more predictable we are as teachers the more our lessons will tend to become routine in the mind of the student. Such an axiom need not be construed as an invitation to capriciousness. Rather it should be a constant challenge to us to try to find new ways of explaining, clarifying, presenting our thoughts to students — especially to those who have worked with us for some length of time.

One of the best stage directors in this country describes his work as one essentially of communicating, to the men and women on stage, concepts which would help them make their characterizations more powerful and convincing. To do this, he contends, one has to explain essentially the same concept a dozen or more times in a dozen or more ways. Such creative communication has to continue until he strikes a point of emotional and intellectual recognition on the part of the actor — the point at which whatever part is being portrayed on stage coalesces with some personal experience. Once that point is reached, the performance becomes convincing; but until that point is reached, the director's job is to try to open up as many different avenues as needed — not repeating the same instructions or using the same illustrations, but rather constantly inventing new ones pointing toward the same end.

Being creative in this way and trying to incorporate a sense of excitement into what we teach can be extremely difficult if the student is not prepared, not receptive, or for whatever reason refuses to participate or respond much beyond a minimal level. Frustration attends our efforts, and very quickly we are apt to subscribe to the attitude that whatever we do will be ineffective and go unheeded by this or that particular student. We may begin to anticipate such a student's lesson with mild displeasure; such continued ineptness tends to irritate us; and we settle back into a kind of dutiful attitude of offering corrections and information, having forsaken much of our imagination or inventiveness.

If such a neutralization takes place, we are guilty of letting the student's attitude determine the atmosphere of the lesson. If the student is bored, hostile, unmusical, sloppy, or whatever, there is no reason why we have to reflect, even in psychological terms, these attitudes. One must make up one's mind that no matter what the effort, at least *one* of us is going to enjoy the lesson. After all, the beauty of the music itself stands before us, and hopefully both student and teacher will be lifted in spirit by attempting to release that beauty.

Like a spiritual leader who believes so strongly in the goodness of the doctrine that the effort to win converts is unceasing, like a doctor who believes so strongly in the value of human life that untiring energy is devoted to lead the sick to healing processes, we must believe so strongly in the fact that music enhances the quality of life that we never let a single opportunity pass to try to show that conviction to a student. Such dedication will not necessarily bring every student around to our point of view, but it will keep our own work vital and an ever-changing challenge. And when we confront ourselves with periodic stocktaking, it is the constant rekindling of this inner flame that is the most important single factor of all, and the means by which we can put other more detailed self-criticisms into proper perspective.

6

Repeated Notes

Practice Procedures

*T*HE subject of practice procedures is one over which serious musicians seem to agonize constantly. As in religion and morality, we feel as if we fall short of ideal standards no matter how good the intentions or how frequent the striving for excellence. We must, in fact, come to the realization that one of our professional hazards is a feeling that we will never completely master the art of efficient learning. But by the same token, we are constantly stimulated by the challenge of improving, and regular reexamination of what we do during that time set aside for practice becomes a way of life.

In the spirit of that reexamination, let us consider three aspects of practice: the balance between confidence and criticism; the maintenance of concentration; and the important points in the learning process at which we need to effect a change of approach.

Confidence in what we do in terms of a day-to-day procedure can be achieved only through learning to strike a balance between criticism of that procedure and a firm, short-term faith that it will indeed produce the results we wish. Without the criticism the procedure might never change, will almost certainly become routine, and a feeling of having gone stale will result. If, however, we criticize our procedure too severely or too constantly, we may never give the procedure a chance to show its effectiveness. Once a given practice technique has been selected, we have to pursue it temporarily with vitality and determination attended by the belief and expectation that what we are doing will indeed "work." The maintenance of a delicate balance between the two poles is thus a necessary requisite for making progress.

Consider for a moment the person who is hypercritical of everything regarding personal practice techniques. The attack on one's self can take place at any point in one's work. Valid ways of practicing, once discovered, are psychologically discarded almost immediately, oftentimes for some essentially irrational reason: "I know so-and-so does a lot of this kind of work, but I just can't seem to sit and do that for hours," or "Such-and-such a technique seems to work for everybody else, but it just doesn't work for me," or "I just don't have the time to work that way," or "Well, I did that every day for a week, but it didn't seem to help."

The cold answer to these irrationalities is simply "why." *"Why* can't you sit and try working that way?" *"Why* won't it work for you if it has worked for others?" *"Why* don't you reschedule your practice time to work in a beneficial way?" Even *"why* didn't you improve after a week of work?" Is it the effectiveness of the technique itself you must doubt? Is it the way in which you carried it out? Or have you selected the wrong practice approach altogether?

There have been a lot of fine performers over the past

years; many of them have left us their practice "secrets" either by writing them down or by leaving them with their students. There is a core of techniques which have the reputation of being efficacious. All of us have had contact with some, if not most, of them; but like moral truths, we sometimes know about them and even recommend them without necessarily living by them ourselves.

When practicing seems out of kilter, it can often be pulled back into focus by giving some truthful and embarrassing answers to oneself. How many times have you repeated the problem area slowly for how many days? How slowly? How many times *after* you've learned the piece do you practice with the same procedure you used *as* you learned the piece (for example, hands separately)? How recently have you taken basic musical components of a piece — phrasing, dynamics, articulation, fingering, or breathing, structure, melodic rise and fall, accentuation — and examined them as separate components to see that you are doing everything indicated on the page? The answers to these questions are usually such that one goes scurrying back to work.

This discussion is not meant to imply that all of us know all the answers but simply do not use them — to be sure, we can always discover a new, helpful way of practice. But it *is* to say that much of the time we do not carry out carefully that which we already know — things that reputedly produce results.

We cannot practice in all ways simultaneously, and oftentimes we choose to practice only one aspect of a piece. Settle within yourself the issue of how you wish to work and how long you will work that way before you can expect to see some results (in terms of time allotted each day for whatever number of days). Then once embarked, don't expect yourself to be doing anything else during that time, and don't keep testing for results. No one ever baked a successful cake by popping open the oven door every five minutes to see if it was going to rise.

During this period, it is best to assume that what you are doing is going to be effective. Doubts can only undermine concentration and lead to an association of psychological disturbance with that particular music. Energy is important during this period. We all realize that a low energy level in carrying out any learning process tends to increase the time needed for results and decrease the sharpness of those results. High energy levels of work, on the other hand, tend to usher in pressure and tension. Energetic practice is possible without excessive stress, but we sometimes have to remember to separate the two.

There do come periodic times to step back from one's work and see what your practice has accomplished. Usually that moment comes only after several days of work at best, sometimes longer. We live in a jet age, and we have become accustomed to expecting fast results. Usually such expectations cannot be applied directly to musical learning or artistic perception. Sometimes something may straighten itself out in a flash, but we can neither depend upon that phenomenon nor force it; and it, too, is more often than not the result of a long period of conscious or subconscious preparation.

When you step back to view your work, you will probably already sense inwardly whether the results are going to be evident. You will often recognize growth, but without complete satisfaction. Such a state may invite you back for another round of the same practice procedure. If you see no improvement whatsoever for your effort, and reexamination of what you have done reveals no apparent lack on your part, then it is indeed possible that you are using the wrong technique to solve this particular kind of problem. Under these circumstances, to be sure, you should either have a brainstorm and try something else, or seek help.

In either case, stocktaking at these intervals should be specific and well thought out. If something is working but just needs more time, fine. But if that something is decidedly not working, then the seeking of other techniques is called for. Open-ended practice of any sort for long periods of time without positive and noticeable improvement can only lead to stalemate. Under the best of circumstances, long, hard practice tends to blunt sharpness of perception and to attenuate concentration.

Concentration

Of all the "magic" words connected with practice, perhaps concentration is the most frequently used, and yet it remains the most elusive. It is a frustratingly paradoxical concept, for if one thinks about concentration (or lack thereof) instead of the work at hand, one is in fact not concentrating. If one's concentration is successful, there will be but dim awareness of this fact while the work goes on. In these paradoxical characteristics, concentrating can be compared to falling asleep (that is, one is not falling asleep as long as one is thinking about or worrying about falling asleep).

Thus one has to approach the act of concentrating somewhat obliquely. And yet one can create conditions conducive to good concentration (just as, once again, one can create conditions conducive to restful sleep). Some of these are obvious: a period of time free from frequent disturbance or interruption; a regularly scheduled period of work so that the entire psyche is eventually programmed into a cycle and into anticipating periods of concentration. Other factors are perhaps more subtle: a positive attitude toward your ability to concentrate and to build up a concentration habit (which includes a willingness to recognize that you are a human being and as such will be subject to fluctuations of concentration for apparently no reason), or the fact that good concentration is closely allied to an approach which constantly seeks to be creative and refreshing.

One's attitude toward concentration is particularly tricky because a belief in the fact that one has poor concentration results in exactly that — poor concentration. As simplistic as it sounds, practicing the reverse also works. Thus a paraphrase of the well-known quotation attributed to Emile Coué can be very helpful: "Every day in every way my concentration gets better and better." This may seem silly, but in fact, feeding the subconscious is of primary importance in building good concentration habits (and incidentally in the control of fear in performance situations, for which concentration is itself the best antidote). Faith in improvement of one's concentrative powers coupled with eternal positiveness will, over a period of months, contribute greatly to the strength and effectiveness of those powers.

Difficult times will of course occur. One's life outside music study goes on. Machinery breaks down, extreme weather generates inconvenience, personal relationships become difficult, temporary illness intervenes, or for no known reason one just doesn't feel like working and can't concentrate. The best way to guide oneself through these rough spots may be different for people of different temperaments. When such situations are rampant, it often results in jumping up from the work at hand every few minutes to attend to this or that, to make that phone call to be sure some household chore has been done. When such symptoms appear, the best solution for me is simply to say something like, "Okay, I can't concentrate today. It all sounds awful and I'm not doing anything constructive. This is a temporary psychological disturbance which will pass, but until it does I will be patient with myself. I will not berate myself, but I will also sit here for the next hour (or however long the practice period is) without interruption. If the phone rings, I won't answer it (they can always call back, and chances are it's not an emergency). If a chore comes to my mind, I'll write it down on a piece of paper close at hand so I won't forget, and I'll do it when my practicing is done. Whatever happens, I'll sit here and try to work. If I get something accomplished, fine. If not, that's also fine."

By thus pointing yourself in this direction with gentle insistence, your concentration will probably begin to return after three or four days, and often when it does, it will surge back with increased strength.

Closely allied to effective concentration is the development of a high degree of variety and creativity in what one does when one practices. Stimulation of our mental processes by changing our focus frequently regenerates mental interest. How one does this is an individual matter, for individual minds are fascinated by different aspects of a given problem, and the list of refocusing devices which one might use to maintain interest is endless. Learning to be creative in this way can act as an effective antidote to the tendency of repetition to deaden attention. When one needs to practice a passage over and over again (which is always the case with difficult passages, much technical work, and even to some extent "easy" sections), one needs to change the procedure every few repetitions. Alter the tempo, play one hand alone while thinking the other, play one hand alone while not thinking the other, think the first two beats and begin playing on the next, listen for inner voices or counter-melodies. The list could go on and on. Each device in itself is not so important as its function in permitting you endless repetition with goal-oriented listening. This constitutes repetition *with* concentration, the kind of drill that should bring benefits.

For many, the most simple kind of change of pace can bring with it new vital concentration. Walter Gieseking, who possessed what must certainly have been one of his generation's most phenomenal abilities to concentrate, used to state that when he found concentration waning, he simply changed to a different style of music for refreshment. In this context it is probably helpful to have three or four different practice areas, involving different musical styles and different learning tasks in a day's practice. It may be helpful to vary the order of these areas from time to time. Most of us have a predilection for "warming up" with technical studies, scales, finger exercises, and so on; but surely these activities can reap a variety of benefits, and studying them sometimes after we are "warmed up" can help us refocus on different goals. By the same token, we are often called upon to perform a composition without suitable warm-up; so by placing such a piece first in a day's practice, we may be able to condition ourselves to focus rapidly and effectively on its musical properties while "cold."

The inventiveness of the mind in creating these small changes in routine, once set upon such a course, will be boundless. It is also obvious that the use of such devices could become excessive and lead to a kind of helter-skelter practice period that would reap few results. Used sparingly and wisely, however, such ideas create a joy and interest in whatever needs to be done; they can ward off the numbing effect of the hard, long hours, the repetition, the drill which is a necessary part of developing superb performance skill.

Technical and Musical Growth

Now let us focus on the broader stages of learning a piece of music and the necessity of changing one's approach from time to time as one progresses through those stages.

The first task which confronts us as we set out to learn a piece of music is what we often call casually "learning the notes." As one approaches this task, prevailing doctrine today suggests that it is advantageous to have an overall concept of what the piece is about. Usually this is not difficult, for either a teacher's performance of the piece, a fellow-student's performance, or a recorded performance is available. It is argued that the student will benefit by having some overall concept of what the eventual goal will be before starting the long, tedious process of learning the piece bit by bit. Such benefits are not to be denied, but we should not rule out the old-fashioned method of just wading in and working in the dark with bits and pieces until it begins to make sense. Such a procedure often leaves one feeling insecure if not totally lost, but there is a spirit of adventure which can be called upon to sustain one's efforts through the toughest initial stages.

The reason this approach, although perhaps not the optimal one, is necessary to keep in one's practice repertoire is that in the case of unrecorded twentieth-century music, it is often the only approach left open. Even visual examination of the score from beginning to end may leave one with only the vaguest of notions of how the piece will actually sound and what the emotional or expressive properties of it actually are (especially if unconventional notation is used). So one is left with only one possible course of action: get started even if you don't know for the moment quite where you are going; regard it as an exploration, an adventure; keep your eyes, ears, and musical responses wide open — that is, take advantage of your lack of preconception by using them as a sensitized antennae eager to pick up the meaning of whatever sound-message emerges. It is possible that philosophical devotion over the past century to the idea of having a whole concept before we begin has resulted in a psychological aversion to the insecurity often encountered in piecemeal learning. In turn, this aversion has made us even more reluctant to tackle difficult contemporary music where — at times — no other course of action is possible. What we must have, of course, is an appreciation for the effectiveness of each approach, each in its own realm.

The drill required in "learning the notes," the efficacy of the experience of having the piece come into our nervous system day by day, provides a kind of reward in itself; the goal of

effective performance seems very reachable, because with careful practice habits, progress is so evident. The pleasure of this
stage is such that it may entice us to work too rapidly, moving
ahead, learning more. Still, it is a "fun" period.

Then suddenly you know the notes, perhaps even having
memorized them, but the piece is not yet ready to be played,
perhaps doesn't sound right or "hang together." The mountain
of achievement which had seemed so near suddenly seems now
to be surrounded by a vast and seemingly endless wasteland,
and often one feels let down with a sense of not knowing quite
what to do next.

First of all, recognize the stage through which one has
passed as preliminary, and understand that real practice begins
only from here on. One must take oneself in hand and institute
a dual procedure. The first one is that of backtracking and
spending time doing the same things you were doing as you
learned the piece, but at a more elementary stage, a lower level
than that of your "best-sounding" playing skill.

As we learned notes we probably practiced at slow tempo,
hands separately, with metronome, in short fragments, made
use of repetition — all those techniques that lead to our first-
stage goal of learning the notes. But once we can play the piece
hands together, at a moderate tempo, with some degree of expression, serious use of first-stage techniques often stops —
except perhaps for an occasional foray to correct a troublesome
passage. Rather, we simply try to improve our performance by
repetition of our moderately skilled playing of the piece. Improvement by this kind of repetition is slow, and often incorpo-
rates problem areas intact into higher stages of performance. As
Cecile Genhart put it, we practice to "perfect imperfection."

What we should do is to practice as if we were learning the
piece carefully for the first time, using first-stage techniques
carefully and regularly, varying them intelligently to ensure
continuing concentration during this phase of our practice.

Even up to the hour of performance, considerable time should be relegated to this kind of careful work.

But, of course, there is another level at which we must continue to develop, for although continuing first-stage techniques will lead to security and greater flexibility of musical expression, such techniques are not an end in themselves and *by themselves* will not necessarily lead to the desired end. The other track we must embark on at this stage is one which can be called a conceptual-musical track. This process consists of studying the piece much as a conductor would. Remember that a conductor cannot practice with live sound all the time. Much of his or her work is done with a score in what appears to be silence. Inside, of course, forces are active both analytically and aurally. Thus the conductor actually thinks about the structure, the concept, the style, the history, the overall effect of a piece, and then practices working with inner sound realization until conceptually a very solid idea is formed of what is sought from a perfect performance of a piece. Then he or she takes this molded concept into orchestral rehearsal, and in very limited amounts of time must convey this personal concept to the players and get them to respond accordingly.

We who are soloists have a distinct advantage because we do not have to wait for the equivalent of an orchestral rehearsal to begin to put our ideas into operation. But we often negate that advantage by simply rushing in to make music without having given the music the requisite conceptual-musical preparation. Too often we try to "correct" or "improve" our performance based on the vague general knowledge that it is not yet "good enough," but we have not thought deeply enough about the music to have formed a clear concept of what it is ideally we seek.

Such knowledge is not always easily achieved. It involves not only the purely musical aspects of the work (for example, structure, dynamics, phrasing, style), but also the emotional or psychological effect which the work should produce in your ideal performance. Moreover, in the case of many works, deep philosophical or spiritual implications are present which one hopes under the best of performance circumstances to impart to the audience.

We have heard it said so many times that music is like language, and we all nod quick assent, but we seldom carry through this analogy to completion. Just as a sentence such as "Where were you last night?" can carry surprise, suspicion, suppressed joy, hostility, or anger, depending on the inflection it receives and the meaning the speaker intends, so can a phrase of music carry an infinite number of subtle emotional meanings depending both on the way in which it is handled musically and *on the intent of the performer.* Too often, for lack of musical-conceptual preparation, we ourselves are not exactly sure of the meaning we intend to convey.

As one approaches the final stage of preparation, the piece begins to want to push ahead by itself, like a pod about to burst into full bloom. Hopefully, it will have achieved a deep technical security, but one which like a garden, will likely have to be tended to some degree constantly by careful first-stage practice. One will continue by the same token to think about the work. To these steps must be finally added the practice of performing the work.

Even with all the preparation in the world, it still takes a special knack to walk right up to the work at a given instant and play it successfully from beginning to end with an ongoing motivation that minimizes mistakes or miscalculations. The work suddenly seems psychologically different somehow when approached this way. Such performances should be practiced, perhaps not every day, but certainly frequently enough in the final stages of preparation so that giving a performance be-comes a comfortable experience. If such a practice becomes too frequent, the details of execution will deteriorate and insecurity will set in, so other types of practice from the earlier stages should be maintained. But unless one indulges in testing one's full capacity for a nonstop performance embodying full emotional, intellectual, and spiritual communication (even to the four walls), one will continue to regard such a pulling together and dispensing of all forces as too rare a happening.

Practice of this type is completely exhausting. After a session of this type one has been so immersed, so concentrated, that one feels almost as if he or she had been on a journey. But being able to induce such deep concentration in the midst of the distraction created by the pressure of an audience is the key to the secret of successful performance. The technique of practicing the handling of such pressure can be perfected by using the imagination to create an audience, a hall, a stage, and at a predetermined time walk to the appropriate spot, bow, and perform. Eventually we can convince ourselves that the physical discomfort of pre-performance nerves (the tiredness, the weakness, the internal pressures, the shortness of breath, the perspiration, however one reacts) does not necessarily mean that the body's responses will be impaired when the instant of performance comes. As a matter of fact, the responses can actually be enhanced. In the practice-performance we cannot create entirely the conditions of real performance, but we can simulate them well enough and often enough so that we begin to trust ourselves in a new way when the moment of performance actually arrives.

7

Ricordanza
(Memory)

Types of Memorizing

*H*ISTORICAL tradition has credited both Franz Liszt and Clara Schumann with being the first to play concerts from memory. Presumably it was part of the virtuoso's stock-in-trade to amaze the audience not only with physical gymnastics but also with intellectual prowess. It may have emerged, too, as virtuoso demands evolved more and more in the direction of using extreme ranges of the keyboard and larger, rapid skips, activities in which visual and spatial awareness could be helpful, thus tending to shift focus away from the score toward the keyboard. Whoever started the trend, since about the middle of the nineteenth century, much solo public performance has been by memory, and the practice is a well-rooted part of our musical culture.

For all its acceptance, however, memorization remains something of a bugaboo. Many young students struggle with it as an added burden after the work of learning the notes has been completed. More advanced students learn to regard it as the final acid test in determining their readiness to perform. Even experienced artists are not immune from either the fear or sometimes the mishap of a memory slip. Memorizing remains hard work, and even after we think we have a piece memorized, the images we store seem to be like malicious phantoms who slip away at the least sign of pressure, but who also linger with surprising clarity when their presence is of no particular consequence.

As a result of the insecurity which often surrounds memorization, areas have been staked out where memory in performance is not necessarily required — chamber music, for example — and even sometimes performance of unusually long, taxing traditional works, such as the "Goldberg" Variations of Bach or complex contemporary works. A few famous artists have learned that they feel more comfortable in public performance with the notes in front of them and have persistently concertized that way, perhaps the most legendary example being Dame Myra Hess. There are, moreover, occasional offensives launched against the practice per se in the form of written or verbal arguments designed to weaken the roots of this tradition.

Why does it continue to persist? Is it really because of the desire to show off one's brain power?

Those who defend memorization do so on the premise that the memory process is, in fact, a technique that has the potential to contribute mightily to the performer's relationships with the music itself. Like all technical tools, its benefit comes with proper use and with a high degree of concentration. One can memorize and have very little realization of the structure or meaning of the music, just as one can practice finger exercises or scales and derive relatively little benefit insofar as basic technical development is concerned. Properly used, however, the memory process can lead to greater understanding of the music, greater conviction about how it should be played, and in the case of certain kinds of temperaments, even greater freedom and flexibility in performance.

One of the most difficult roles to define in terms of the memory process is that of the practiced muscular response to memorized signals. When a child first begins to memorize, it is this muscular response which will probably be relied upon. The young performer can play this piece "by heart" because a process has been learned which is essentially physical in nature and is triggered by some kind of cue (inner hearing; remembering the image of a page; seeing relative positions of black and white keys on a keyboard; and even remembering finger numbers). One or more of these cues may with practice be reduced to a mere shred of an image so that the physical response becomes increasingly automatic and the mind less likely to follow through after having given its initial "start" impulse.

This all works fine until the moment of public performance arrives. Then, of course, the awkwardness which attends our physical actions when we are under close scrutiny begins to interfere with the normal pattern of muscular response. The response falters or stops. The triggering cue may be several measures back, and there is nothing to fall back on in terms of mental support. The only alternative is to go back and refire the cue, with the hope that momentum will carry through the muscular responses this time. Very likely the trauma of having faltered or stopped will, however, work against the momentum, and similar faltering or stopping will occur at or before the same spot. If this happens, the only other solution is to find another cue farther along, usually at the beginning of the next section or near the end of the piece.

The pattern just described is familiar to all of us. Our

antidote as teachers is to tell the student that one can't depend on the muscular response (pianists say "can't depend on your fingers") but that one has to "know" the piece.

Such advice may be as good as an antidote to a given situation, but a successful memory habit is really a delicate balance of a number of facets, and one of those *is* in fact good muscular response. Overdoing the intellectual approach can be as devastating as its opposite. Let us suppose that the student takes this advice and is motivated to study every aspect of a given piece completely, having been totally convinced by the breakdown trauma and the teachers' advice that muscular response can't be trusted under pressure. The very intensity of the anti–memory-lapse campaign will give credence to the lapse, and when the music becomes difficult enough to demand the playing of passages where muscles have to take over, an abundance of intellectual cues will interfere. It's the old story of asking the centipede which leg goes before which.

Thus there are students (and this syndrome usually comes at the intermediate or college level) who can write out their pieces; who can start at any one of a number of overlapping sections, who can cite harmonic and structural data until it comes out of their ears, but who still tremble at the prospect of a memorized performance and who may continue to break down, although they can now retreat to a nearby pickup cue. Even if they manage successful continuity, they will still feel emotionally inhibited by the very process of keeping the music on the track. It is, of course, this uncomfortable situation which leads to despair and bitterness with regard to playing from memory.

Often, discussions of memorizing center around the relative values of various types of mental activity. There are those, for example, who place the activity of inner hearing (the "ear") above all other types of concentration. That the ear should be developed to as high a level as possible is certainly true, but in reality there are few musicians who are gifted to the extent that they can literally play whatever they hear inwardly, even after years of training. Working against the ear also are the facts that in music of extreme virtuosity, complex patterns of notes have to be played with great speed sometimes, and in both music of highly dissonant or contrapuntal nature, a multitude of difficult relationships may exist virtually simultaneously. The ear may very well be the most important single intellectual activity, but it cannot be the entire story. It is perhaps significant in this regard that musicians who can improvise brilliantly, and who thus rely heavily on their ear, do not necessarily memorize preexisting music easily.

Visual memory of the page is a highly personal thing. It seems to be an activity of the brain which one either tends to use by nature or not. Those who have total recall, or "photographic memory," as it's often called, are presumably to be envied. If you can carry your music in your mind, isn't it as good as having it up there on the music rack? Apparently not. In many cases, people with "photographic memories" under normal circumstances find that their concentration too is disturbed by pressure. The necessity of maintaining continuity during performance is still frightening. Should a breakdown occur, they can always revisualize the page and get going again, but by then the flow is broken and the damage has been done. This fear may not be true of all musicians gifted with "photographic memory," but it is true of many, so that often such performers seek to add to their visual memory strong support from other areas.

Spatial-tactile memory is an activity which is closely akin to muscular memory, but one in which the mind concentrates on the "feel" of the motions involved in playing the instrument and the tactile sensations involved in touching the instrument. Like visual memory, its use is somewhat individual, but those whose propensity is to use it seem to laud it. The fact that it is akin to the area of muscular response makes it dangerous without supplemental activity, but such closeness is also its strength in that it reinforces the muscular response in such a way as to result in a good sense of security.

Finally comes the old standby of theoretical and structural analysis. As a technique, it is the most universally recommended and should never be neglected. Its limitations, however, make it valuable as a strong supplemental technique rather than as a central one. Such limitations are born of the fact that focus on these aspects can easily act as inhibiting factors to good muscular response in performers. Also, knowing and understanding these aspects of the music, while extremely valuable in assessing the expressive content of a piece, are nonetheless not synonymous with that content and do not ensure reaction to it either on the part of the performer or the audience. Furthermore, in much twentieth-century music, theoretical or structural analysis becomes so complex as to be useless in the heat of performance.

It thus becomes fairly apparent that out of these activities, most should be utilized and developed to some extent in conjunction with drilled muscular response if successful memorized performance is to come about. The balance of such activities will likely be an individual matter, but some measure of each needs to be present.

Memorizing for Performance

One of our most frequent mistakes is to attribute to memory failure the muscular tie-up which sometimes takes place under pressure. Faulty memory can indeed cause that tie-up, but so can other things. If one blames memory when, in fact, one's memory checks out solidly upon examination, then other factors should also be examined. Questions could be asked with regard to fingering; has the passage been drilled enough for security, so that it feels good in a tactile sense in practice sessions? Does it need to be divided differently from a mental standpoint, to enhance mental clarity and muscular facility? Is the passage rhythmically solid, so that pulse and accent do not accelerate unconsciously?

Such questions may seem to beg the solution of the memory problem. But not really. Memory can only provide the proper mental images and start the proper series of muscular responses, retriggering in sequence as the piece is played. It cannot act as a substitute for proper or sufficient preparation.

The key here is "proper or sufficient." Most of us know about "proper." We know *what* needs to be done in terms of slow, careful practice, using various time-honored techniques (such as rhythmic variations, repetition at various speeds; hands separately). What often escapes us is *how much*.

A passage, once drilled, seems to be secure, and so we stop our drill work. It stays secure apparently, and we think no more about it. Then when the time comes to perform, it is discovered to be woefully insecure and perhaps even disastrous. *Pressure* is the unknown factor. Inexperienced performers always underestimate its power to disturb concentration and muscular response. It can be overridden, but sometimes it takes bullheaded determination almost to the point of doggedness.

We can point to a number of activities in which hard drilling programs are used in such a way that even in the face of pressure or extreme trauma, a given response is so ingrained that it will be carried out. Military training is often so rigorous that given responses will be executed as a matter of survival under life-threatening conditions. The response is so propelled by determination that decisions can be made, plans altered, diverse tactics used, and goals aggressively realized. At the time this action takes place, fear is thrust aside, and the battle against it is momentarily won.

Once having put on the steam in this way and made progress, there is a strong probability it will be easier next time
around. Or to put it another way, if you've kicked fear in the
teeth once and got away with it, the spirit of the demon will
probably not be as strong the next time and, given similar
circumstances, victory over it won't be quite as hard.

Memory is a muscle, it has often been said. We repeat the
catch phrase, but often we do not carry the analogy far enough.
If memory is a muscle, then we must apply to memory development the same rigors we would apply to muscular development.
If we wanted more flexible, stronger muscles, we would expect
to spend time every day working with them. Do we spend time
consciously memorizing every day? Most of us would have to
confess to memorizing only when we need to, but not as a
normal part of our daily practice schedule. Taking fifteen to
thirty minutes per day for memorizing will do wonders.

Memorizing does not, of course, mean just repeating a
section of a piece over and over again until one can play it
without the notes. It does mean:

- Examining every line intervalically; concentrating on its sound
  and its theoretical reference framework (major or minor scale?
  mode? tone row?); thinking the line without playing or singing
  it; then thinking it while playing or singing it.
- Examining vertical structures both stated and implied. Find basic chord progressions and play them in several keys as progressions per se. When chords are implied, such as would occur in
  solo unaccompanied lines or in earlier keyboard music, such as
  where a single note or two in the bass implies a full harmony
  which is not stated, find and play full chords to impress upon
  your harmonic consciousness what is really going on. In this
  context it is oftentimes helpful (and fun) to make an arrangement
  of the music, using basic harmonic and melodic materials much
  as if you were using it as a basis for improvisation. Do not be

shocked at such tampering. It has a distinguished history, for Bach, Mozart, Beethoven, Liszt, and most nineteenth-century composers were expert at the techniques. The only difference is that today we don't play our paraphrases in public.

- Examining the music away from the instrument both as an object for pondering and as a way of testing your aural recall; you should try to sing or play the music in clear relief mentally, without actually making a sound.

- Testing yourself constantly by stopping and restarting in awkward places, by backing up. Stop in the middle of playing something and continue only mentally for, say, two bars, then pick up the thread in performance again.

Difficult and time consuming? Yes, but as one works with such techniques every day, they become less difficult and less time-consuming. If one sets a fixed amount of time for such work, at first it won't seem as if one gets very far. After a few weeks, however, one will find it is possible to forge ahead in the allotted time.

One last caution. Do not spread yourself thin by moving ahead in memorizing a piece until the first task you set for yourself is done. If one works, say, fifteen minutes on two measures one day and they seem memorized, one begins with exactly the same two measures the next day. In all probability the memory images will have faded. Don't just polish them up and move on. Rather begin building from the bottom once again, repeating every drill, going through every step, every stage. Probably it will only take you ten minutes instead of fifteen. That leaves five minutes to begin work on the next section. The next day begin once again at the first section; maybe today will take you only five minutes to do those drills, and you can spend ten minutes on the second section. Leave the first section unpracticed only on the day after you can play or sing that section with complete security, coming on it absolutely cold. Then skip practicing it for a day and work on other sections. After a day away, return to it and check it. Drill it a bit. Once it is secure again, you may be able to leave it for two days before rechecking and drilling, and so on.

Once memorizing becomes a regular part of one's routine, it becomes one of the most fascinating and pleasurable parts of the day's practice. In time it will lead to the kind of security which makes whether or not to play a memorized performance a moot question, for one is just as comfortable without the music as with it.

8

Pour les Trois Pedales . . .

*T*EACHING pedaling is at least as complex a matter as teaching basic finger technique. As with the teaching of any technique, opinions will vary as to the most desirable aesthetic for which to strive and the most effective method to achieve that goal. Discussion of pedaling is not so much a matter of answering those questions by proffering a single point of view, but rather of focusing on the very questions themselves, thereby bringing into clearer relief the importance of the use of the pedals as a factor in determining the final result.

The Damper Pedal

Beethoven was the first master composer to indicate the use of the damper pedal extensively, and in so doing left us with a series of pedal problems. His blurring of the recitative lines in the Op. 31 no. 2, the mixing of tonic and dominant harmonies in the last movement of the Op. 53 and in the Fifth Piano Concerto simply do not square with the generally accepted practices of harmonic clarity. We have thus to explain this re-peated penchant in some way which lets us off the hook.

One theory is that Beethoven's hearing had deteriorated to the point where he didn't realize the folly of his pedal indica-tions. Not likely. Beethoven's *inner* hearing became even more acute as his aural awareness of the outer world diminished, and the inner voices which produced the miracles of the late years could hardly be so remarkably sensitive on one hand and so inept on the other. Furthermore the second movement of the relatively early B-flat major Piano Concerto, Op. 19, presents an example of similar mixing of harmonies we usually consider incompatible. It was written well before his hearing had proba-bly started to fail to any great extent.

We have, rather, to accept the fact that Beethoven was fond of the color which resulted from mixing harmonies, even tonic and dominant ones, and that this coloration was behind his thinking rather than the use of the pedal as a device to connect lines or harmonies.

Assuming such a mixture still seems too ripe today for many ears, we can next begin to take into consideration the differences between the sonorities of the late-nineteenth- and twentieth-century piano and those of pianos of earlier times. We can also add to the mix various experimental phases through which pedals themselves went: multiple pedals or those which split the keyboard into upper and lower registers with separate sonority controls.

If we combine the concepts of Beethoven's interest in a certain amount of color mix and the moderated sonority of early instruments, we are brought face to face with the necessity of adapting our pedal technique in some way to include both; that is, some mixing, but not as much as today's pianos will offer if we depress the pedal fully.

Such thinking throws many into a quiet panic as they begin

to contemplate the necessity of using the pedal in some way other than as an on-off switch. We must, however, gear ourselves up to entering the twilight zone of half-tint, using the pedal on a continuum with multiple "positions," much as we use a volume control, a dimmer switch, or the accelerator of a vehicle.

Such a concept begins to be valuable if used in addressing many pedaling problems. For example, if one examines original early-nineteenth-century editions of virtuoso piano music, one often encounters longer pedals for arpeggation, chromatic scales, or other figuration than we are accustomed to using for desired clarity. Or if we look at long pedal indications in the form of written-out long-note bass sonorities in much music at the turn of the twentieth century, we are once again confronted with a need for some measure of adjustment. Careful voicing and balance can improve clarity but are not the complete answer. We are still confronted with the necessity of entering that twilight zone of half-pedaling or half-damping.

The reason we are so uncomfortable with such half-tint pedaling is, of course, that we never develop it, teach it, or experiment with it. This is not surprising, in that most of the pedaling we see marked by editors is notated with the assumption that the pedal is either up or down, with the dampers either totally off the strings or damping them to complete silence.

In order to enter this coloristic world of half-tint we need to realize that we control the pedal by aural image and feedback, just as we control touch, phrasing, and dynamic levels, that "correct" pedaling for one set of acoustical parameters may not work for the next, that pedal response differs from piano to piano (like action), that adjustments in voicing and balance have profound effect on pedaling, and that constant attentiveness to the overall sonority is the key to maintaining the desired mix as well as to providing small, ongoing corrective adjustments.

Physical training of the foot might begin with observing at exactly what level of depression the dampers begin to leave the strings. On most pianos the level will be surprisingly near the top of the range of pedal action. The amount of release from this position which is needed to effect damping is usually extremely small. Somewhere in the middle of this small range of action is a level in which the dampers are but partially in contact with the strings, providing some, but not complete, dampening. Learning to operate comfortably in this small range and sensitizing one's foot to its control is a necessary basic technique.

The aural awareness which is fundamental to developing this approach to pedaling must be practiced with faithful regularity. Exercises for developing it might include practicing scales with pedal in such a way that the use of pedal is undetectable except when it is removed altogether (at which point previously luminous, legato scalework will suddenly sound more dry and clattery). Holding bass pedal points through two or three harmonic changes by a series of quick half-dampings is another exercise.

Independence of foot action from rhythmic accentuation and finger release is another aspect of pedal technique which needs practice. One can devise simple exercises in which the foot must come up at various designated points in a rhythmic or pulse pattern. One might practice releasing on the second of four sixteenth notes, then the third. Notice the difference. Almost immediately when patches of clarity are injected in a texture of passage-work, the effect of suddenly clarity, even for an instant, is so potent that the overall impression is one which allows some pedal in passages which it would seem otherwise inappropriate to pedal. Learning to time foot action to leave these clear patches may be problematic, however, because most of us have a deep-seated habit of "changing" the pedal in such a way that repedaling immediately becomes a reflex action. Thus simply releasing it with the repedaling action delayed by a note or two may be quite new from a muscular standpoint and accordingly very difficult.

Once again an examination of early-nineteenth-century editions suggests to us that leaving these "clear" spots was common practice, and that habitual instant repedaling probably came about with the advent of syncopated or legato pedaling as the pedal became increasingly used as an alternative to finger legato.

These indications must be regarded as possible clues in a historical puzzle which will undoubtedly never be solved. First of all, the possibility looms large that typesetting was not as refined or careful as accurate research might hope for, not to mention outright errors. Quite aside from the printing process, however, is the notational practice itself. When Beethoven, for example, notated the opening bars of the Op. 31 no. 2, he combined pedal with a portato touch notation. Thus portato without pedal might suggest a sliver of actual silence between notes, but *with* pedal the silence is gone, and we are left with a sustained touch form, still portato and still different from either staccato or legato, but no longer containing silence as an ingredient. This combination opened the way to a host of ambiguities, and soon we encounter pedaled (i.e., sustained) staccato notes and even rests. The validity of such combinations cannot be challenged because they represent some concept of sound, sonority, and texture in the minds of the composers. But the system of notation is so ambiguous as to invite several possible realizations without the possibility of knowing for sure which the composer might have had in mind.

As the nineteenth century progressed, fascination with large, complex sound combinations continued to grow as composers both dealt in more heavily altered harmonies and also explored the limits of sonority of which the piano seemed capable. Mixing harmonic elements by using longer pedals became commonplace, as did using the various registers of the keyboard with the pedal to imitate orchestral textures. This coloristic approach reached its zenith with music written at the turn of the century and continued in the works of more "Romantic" composers right on through the twentieth century. Notwithstanding the enormous increase in amount, subtlety, and sensitivity in the use of the pedal suggested by both the music and the performance tradition, the basic method of notating the use of the pedal remained the same, continuing to direct simplistically that the pedal was either "on" or "off."

What did happen, however, is that the symbolism was shifted away from the beat to the delayed, syncopated changing. The downbeat, once the usual time to put the pedal down, became instead the time to release the pedal, thus cleaning the preceding harmony, and repedaling immediately before the keys are released. The effect is, of course, to create a connected sound base which, if carefully handled in terms of key attacks and releases, can simulate legato. The effect was so useful, especially in the context of using extreme ranges of the instrument, that this technique virtually supplanted every other approach.

This so-called "syncopated" or "legato" pedaling still remains the basic technique which is taught in the studio. It still serves a host of situations admirably. Unfortunately it has also reduced us into leaving a great number of other useful techniques unattended, if not badly neglected. Thus finger legato is seldom practiced with diligence today. On-the-beat pedaling has been all but forgotten, half-pedaling remains relatively unexplored, and pedaling with rhythmic precision to create "clear" spots is seldom developed.

Teachers need to investigate a much larger menu of basic pedaling techniques, and time needs to be spent training both the foot and the aural perception of the overall texture. Doing so will add another whole dimension of expressive individuality to performances and will make the perception and playing of the late-nineteenth and twentieth-century literature a great deal more accessible.

how to play softly unless one discards this crutch. At the other end are those who recommend its use constantly, calling attention to the change in tone color which accompanies its use, at least on the grand piano where a fewer number of strings are actually activated when it is depressed. Those who listen for this change of color do not regard the *una corda* as a device for producing softer sound, but rather as a way to refresh the ear with a "new" timbre. In line with this way of thinking, advice may be given to use the *una corda* and project through its diminished intensity, playing *mezzo-forte* or louder. Scriabin probably had this kind of effect in mind on the opening page of the F-sharp minor sonata, Op. 23, when he calls for the *una corda* in conjunction with a dynamic level of *forte*.

In the everyday world of the practice-room cubicle, the *una corda* is often employed as a defense against the incessant raw sound of hammers hardened by many hours of use. In such situations, the left foot may be conditioned to be very quick to jump in and rescue the ear against unwanted harshness. Such a habit can develop into virtually a reflex action, even on a piano where it is no longer needed, and as such can cripple the ability to develop sound-control technique.

On the other hand, a useful trick may be used to take the edge off of the sound of a concert instrument which has hammers grooved by heavy use. The *una corda* may be pressed down just enough to shift the hammers away from contacting the strings with their grooved ruts, so that they strike the strings with fresh felt. Usually pressing the *una corda* pedal only a fraction of its range of depression will give the desired effect, without shifting the hammers so far as to lose contact with the normal number of strings. Since such a balance can be maintained only by fixing the foot in an intermediate position, it very probably will induce fatigue in the ankle or leg. Its use may have to be selective if the playing time on this instrument is lengthy.

The danger of the use of the *una corda* pedal emerges, then, as one succumbs to frequent reflex action rather than maintaining thoughtful aural perception and discriminating touch. As a tool with which to color cantabile lines or harmonic mix, the *una corda* can be highly evocative and belongs with the damper pedal in its potential to add interest and beauty to the sonority. But also like the damper pedal, its use must be planned, and its effects must be evaluated constantly by attentive aural perception.

9

Balancing Act

Subjectivity versus Objectivity

NO one has to make a case for the power of psychological conditioning these days. From our first college course in basic psychology where we read about Pavlov and his dogs to the plots of about half of our TV or movie theater thrillers, the case for the fact that the mind can be conditioned to respond a certain way to given stimuli is overwhelming. Even if we set aside the limitations of laboratory experiments, we would probably agree that we are constantly being "conditioned" in everyday living. We build likes and dislikes, expectations, both good and bad, and reactions over the years. These solidify into concepts which, taken as a whole, can be construed as a kind of philosophy of life.

The interesting part is that, for many of us, that philosophy of life is formed out of a series of haphazard events which happened early in the game. We are conditioned by a series of coincidences or random events, or we hear of others' experiences, and we reach certain conclusions. Later, after our philosophy has been formed, we are even prone to selecting those facts which fit that philosophy and rejecting or ignoring those that don't. Maintaining our philosophy becomes more important to us than maintaining objectivity. Being "right" about life becomes more important than really discovering truth.

Determining objective truth in metaphysical terms is a problem which has plagued thinkers from the beginning of time. In the opinion of many, there is no metaphysical "truth" which will cover all situations. But it is possible to conceive of relatively more objective perception as opposed to subjective perception. Probably most of us have areas in which subjectivity seems the more important. Our society conditions us to those areas in many instances. For example, we live in a social order where "being in love" is construed to be a highly subjective thing. Subjectivity in this matter is considered to be desirable. Thus arranged marriages are considered to be unfeeling, and marrying the person of one's dreams is considered exciting. The fact that the person of one's dreams turns out to be quite different oftentimes from the flesh-and-blood spouse underscores the weakness of subjectivity, for it can lead us into difficulty. On the other hand, no one gets very rhapsodic over a courtship which is planned with only financial, genetic, or power structures in mind. Such considerations seem somehow to rob one of the exhilaration and the ecstasy associated with love and marriage.

Nowhere is it more important to strike a balance between the two concepts of subjectivity and objectivity than in making music. When a performer goes too far in the direction of subjectivity, capriciousness and instability result. On the other hand, when one regards music totally with an eye toward perceiving objectively what is there on the page, and as a result blocks off subjective response, dullness results at worst and mediocrity at best.

Historically, the pendulum has reached the extremes of both sides of the swing during the twentieth century. This century came in at a time when subjectivity was highly prized in many quarters. Philosophy of the nineteenth century had prepared the way by centering on individual emotional response to artistic stimuli. Topics which suggested sweeping consequences and "grand" emotions were popular: love, death, salvation, destiny, for example. Plunging in and being saturated with such emotions was more important than the printed plan which served as a guide, that is, the musical score. Busoni, who was considered unusually objective and rational as a musician, spends several pages in his *Aesthetics* telling us how woefully inadequate the score becomes when one compares it with the spirit behind the creative idea. The suggestion is that one should be free with the score as long as one is elucidating the spirit.

Excessive tampering at the turn of the twentieth century led to distortions so grotesque that the spirit was destroyed, in the opinion of many. The reactions set in, and "follow the score" became the watchword of teachers, students, and many performers. The rise of musicology called our attention to the study of historical performance practices, and soon objective study and research were almost synonymous with great art. Even at the height of this wave, exceptions were allowed — revered artists who obviously treated the music in a highly personal manner: Rachmaninoff, Rubinstein, Horowitz, or Kreisler. Often they were of an age which retained much of the nineteenth-century tradition.

Still, many younger musicians rallied around the more objective approach insofar as their own work was concerned. They worked hard, did their research, and presented their case

in performance. They were thus quite surprised to find themselves often greeted with complaints such as "everyone sounds
alike these days" or "everybody's good these days, but no one
inspires." Soon many regarded the past as a "golden age" which
was rife with performances no one today could approach.

Little by little, over the past decades many musicians
trained in the objective procedure have been relaxing their devotion to it. They have become sophisticated enough to realize
that slavish devotion to the score may not be the only approach
to study. Some composers were careful and accurate in notation, and others much less so. Some composers were temperamentally geared to the concept of an abstract ideal insofar as
performance of their music was concerned; others probably
never conceived of such an ideal and, indeed, were more prone
toward an improvisatory regard for all music. Many have begun
to rethink the matter of subjectivity in dealing with music.
Legend attributes to Pablo Casals the saying: "The notes on the
page are not important, rather what's between the notes." One
must somehow attempt both to integrate and to balance one's
personal emotional response to the music with a more objective
study of its musical and historic aspects.

The difficulty in striking a balance is that once one becomes wedded to a given emotional profile, once our overall
mood-tone has been set and the details of nuance unfold in
patterns we cherish, we tend to become very set in our opinion
as to just how a piece should sound. The positive benefit of this
is that it leads to conviction and authority, the ability to sell a
concept even to those who may regard the music differently.
The negative benefit is, however, that one can become stubbornly immersed in one's beliefs to the exclusion of both stylistic insights unveiled by historical research and even further
development of one's own creativity with regard to the music.

Striking the balance between working objectively and subjectively often requires two quite different working methods. By temperament and training, each of us will first naturally lean in one direction or another. Whichever one it is, we have to condition ourselves to change the mode of approach from time to time. If subjective response comes first, then having to settle down after a while and work carefully is a matter of discipline and slowing down the flow of emotional reaction. One has to condition oneself to think, to evaluate, and to achieve control. Then you can go back to your natural feeling with new insight. If, on the other hand, your first stage of study is to analyze, to check expression marks, to work carefully and slowly, you must after a time, stop yourself, step back, listen inwardly to the piece, and condition yourself to begin to rev up emotionally until you feel the emotional flow bringing you to a response of real excitement. Once you understand and feel such a response, then you can enhance your careful work by having learned to call up the emotional elements. Either way, it is a matter of conditioning yourself during your practice time over many days, so that you gain flexibility in achieving the balance between subjective excitement and objective fidelity to the music you perform.

Working against the grain of our natural bent is valuable technique with which to balance out the excessive bents of students. The student whose music making is emotionally responsive to the point of losing discipline and optimum coherence can thus be guided to a consideration of the values of the written page by working creatively with a strong allegiance to every written direction, a detailed consideration of compositional devices and structural relationships, and an in-depth regard for the appropriate historic performance practice. The student who responds to all of that detail but whose final product is somehow devoid of personal emotional excitement must be fired through relating all of this to the basic emotional drive of the music, the composer's impulse in creating it, and how they relate to emotional experiences from the performer's experiences in living.

One might argue as to which direction is more resistant to the teacher's urgings. Some would vote for the sometimes onerous task of taming the free spirit in such a way that wildness becomes artistic beauty. Others would point to the difficult task of lighting the fire of inspiration in the cool regard of intellectual consideration. Success is possible in both cases, and although the basic temperament of a musician can perhaps never be wholly altered, each can come to understand and apply the process by which their native gifts can be enhanced by artificially inseminating elements of their temperamental opposite.

Performance Practice

Most piano teachers are respectful of the entire area of performance practice, and given a reasonable degree of flexibility are willing to make an honest, sustained effort to move in the direction of intelligent, consistent application of practices which are supported by historical evidence. In the past fifty years, teachers have become much more sophisticated about good editions, for example. Most teachers seek out either urtext editions or critical editions in which the composer's markings are clearly distinguishable from editorial realizations and other performance suggestions. Most teachers have definite concepts with regard to the appropriate use of pedals, realization of ornaments, and even the aesthetic parameters which are suggested by the historic fix of the music. Most realize, too, that continued study and research will bring to light new evidence which, in turn, will be the basis for further consideration in present-day realization of music from the past.

On the other hand, we have to face up honestly to the fact

that there are limits, that we will probably never go far enough in our efforts to re-create past styles for those who are purists, and that even though we may be faulted for only going part of the way in the quest for authenticity, we are, in fact, the principal link through which most of that music will continue to live. Thus, defining both our position and its strengths or weaknesses will hopefully relieve us from that vague sense of guilt which emerges when matters of authenticity are broached and which often undermines our best efforts. Knowing where we stand will not render us free from criticism, but at least we can be clear about out own aesthetic parameters, and then we can do our best within those boundaries to be true to the letter and the spirit of the music we play.

In this context, the largest issue is the use of the modern piano itself for literature written before its development to its present state. The controversy surrounding this issue became heated when, in the mid-twentieth century, performance practices of the eighteenth century became the focus of a great deal of musicological research. The clamor against the distortions of nineteenth-century editorial practices as applied to music of the eighteenth century extended to the use of the instruments themselves. Thus as we pianists discontinued our use of nineteenth-century editions of early music, pressure was also brought to discontinue playing eighteenth-century music on the piano.

Many pianists who had focused extensively on eighteenth-century repertoire were thus put in the position of either giving up the piano as their primary instrument, redirecting their attention to a later segment of the literature, or fighting back. Some chose indeed to stand their ground and argue that a careful look at eighteenth-century performance practice suggests that choice of instrument for the music at hand was a flexible issue, and that an extension of that principle would suggest that the piano might well be included in the family of keyboard instruments on which the music could be played.

Others were influenced to eschew performing eighteenth-century music in public for fear of drawing adverse criticism, and they limited their use of such literature to the teaching studio.

Those pianists who did brave the opposition and continued to play eighteenth-century music on the piano did so by making adjustments in the direction of appropriate performance practice: ornamentation was cleaned up and expanded, pedaling was limited to careful, appropriate enhancement of textures, and an attempt was made to bring articulation more in line with the variety of nonlegato touches used in the period. Purists were never mollified by their attempts, but many keyboard players have become comfortable with this compromise. (A comparison might be made in the world of drama where we accept the fact that conversation between foreigners in their native country takes place in English, an unlikely choice of language, but necessary, given the fact that an English-speaking audience needs to be able to understand it. Then compensation for the improbability is interjected by having the actors simulate a foreign accent!)

Having thus been forced to a middle-ground compromise with regard to eighteenth-century music, pianists soon became aware that purists were advancing even further, for later twentieth-century research began to focus on the remarkable qualities of the early piano. Present-day builders were able to re-create various models of pianos of the late eighteenth and very early nineteenth centuries. Thus the experts began to urge pianists to give up playing Haydn, Mozart, and Beethoven on modern pianos. Most pianists, indeed, would agree that studying performances of literature of the period on period instruments is enlightening and beneficial. But giving up such a large segment of a literature which tradition accorded to today's pianos for so many years is very difficult. So, most pianists prefer to return to today's piano with adjustments which purport to enhance the appropriate aesthetic environment, preferring to compromise rather than to give up the instrument they love.

The purists will continue to complain, pushing their hopes for a world devoid of aesthetic distortion, as they conceive it. From their camp we hear now that today's piano is appropriate only for music written after Brahms, and that performances of all the nineteenth-century "piano" composers, including Schubert, Chopin, Liszt, Schumann, and Brahms, are best left to those who are able to seek out period pianos or present-day recreations. In the work-a-day world of the profession, it is clear that pianists are not going to give up their Scarlatti and Bach, much less Haydn, Mozart, and Beethoven, and certainly not the nineteenth-century composers. Most will be content to live thus with their shortcomings (if, indeed, they *are* shortcomings), do what can be done to refine perceptions of the practices and aesthetics of history, and make appropriate adjustments on the pianos at hand. Some will cry "cop out." But our defense is that we continue to honor the music by studying it, loving it, and playing it intelligently. We cannot all possess and maintain a battery of period instruments, but we *can* attempt to use what instruments we do own with sensitivity when we adapt older music to it.

(An interesting attempt is currently being made to use MIDI-controlled synthesizers to simulate period instruments, and, indeed, carefully sampling can teach us a great deal about the sounds of those instruments. Without, however, re-creating the mechanical aspect, the physical process to activate and control those sounds is apt to differ so widely from that of the historic instruments themselves that the resulting educational value is limited. Computer technology, being the powerful force it is, will very likely solve the problem of simulating various older keyboard actions very soon.)

10

Contemporary Challenge

A Case for the Defense

AS teachers and performers, we are constantly being
scolded for our unwillingness to get involved more deeply
in contemporary music. We are called anachronisms even when
we weakly offer our teaching and playing of Bartók or Pro-
kofieff as evidence of activity in twentieth-century areas. The
case for the plaintiff is unquestionably strong, and since it is
presented forcefully and frequently, we seem not to recognize
that there are some fallacies in it. We seem to forget that a case
for the defense exists at all. Let us consider the fallacies in the
plaintiff's case for a few moments, and in doing so, perhaps we
can come to terms with some of the problems involved in dealing with contemporary music.

First of all, those who urge us to get involved in contemporary music usually use the term "contemporary" in a highly selective sense. What they usually mean is music of the twentieth century which in some way uses what we often call avant garde materials. These materials may include music written in nontonal, twelve-tone, or serial styles; music which relies heavily on disjunct, fragmented textures: music which is rhythmically complex, often highly irregular in terms of traditional pulse, and occasionally that which employs mathematically irrational time values; music which is aleatory; or music which uses the piano in some other way than playing on the keys (for example, plucking, scraping, or strumming, often with the help of various objects such as erasers, screws, paper clips, or thimbles).

By thus using "contemporary" to mean this special type of music, the plaintiff automatically discounts or ignores much music which is in fact part of the contemporary scene. For example, we all know of a vast body of recently composed music which is intended to be used as instructional material and which is based primarily on eighteenth- and nineteenth-century concepts of harmony, rhythm, melody, and texture. This music is useful as a guide for students until they can deal directly with the masters of those centuries.

Moreover, quite aside from didactic materials, there exists a large repertoire of music by composers of the twentieth century who have chosen to continue to use — in updated form — time-honored concepts. In the eyes of the plaintiff, we may score a couple of points higher than the Bartók-Prokofieff stage if we play and teach this group, but such activity doesn't really raise our stock appreciably. The result is that many accomplished composers seem to count for little: certainly the entire Russian school such as Kabalevsky or Shostakovitch, Americans such as Copland, Barber, Lees, Muczynski, or Persichetti, South Americans such as Villa-Lobos or Ginastera; Europeans such as Poulenc, Martin, or Martinů; and a sizeable segment of the British group such as Britten, Leighton, or Ferguson, as well as virtually all of the Spanish school.

Now, granted that this large body of music stands as the conservative side of the twentieth-century scene and much of it was written before 1950, it nevertheless should not be put down so easily as not being representative of contemporary musical thought. There is, after all, a great deal of significant music by well-known composers in this category. Much of it is expertly written, and although it has no guarantee of survival for generations to come, neither has any music of our time.

The second point in analyzing the plaintiff's case is that which assumes that the avant garde music which is endorsed has a right to be heard, and that if not understood or liked immediately, repeated hearing will bring enlightenment and a change of viewpoint on the part of the listener. Let us deal with each point separately.

If someone suggests that new music has the right to be heard simply because it is new, the suggestion really implies the right to be heard in public performance. Preparation of new music for public performance takes time, and a musician's working time is worth money, just as anyone else's. Thus an investment in the preparation of a new work for performance is a very real one. If, after a new score has been scrutinized by the performer, the investment seems worthwhile, then fine; but if it does not seem worthwhile in the opinion of the performer, then there should be absolutely no obligation on the part of the performer to prepare and play the work in the name of its having a "right" to be heard.

No one would expect that every newly written play has a "right" to be produced, or that every new novel has a "right" to be published. Producing plays and publishing novels cost money, and if a producer or publisher invests in a new work, it is because they believe in the work — either in commercial or artistic terms. To expect performers to prepare and play new works simply to get them heard is to devalue the performer's time and effort. Like the producer and the publisher, the performer should have every reason to expect that his or her investment in terms of time and effort will result in successful return — the performer thinking almost always in artistic terms and perhaps those of enhancing his or her professional reputation.

Now turning to the point that repeated hearing will bring enlightenment and appreciation for a new work, it must be pointed out that this is at best but a half-truth. Historical evidence of famous works having received notoriously bad first receptions can be counterbalanced with examples of masterworks having been accepted on first hearing with great enthusiasm. We have to realize also that the beginnings of that vein of twentieth-century music which has traveled through the decades under the avant garde banner began in earnest more than three-quarters of a century ago. Looking back with this perspective, we can see strong works of the avant garde and weak works. Repeated hearings can only underscore the measure of intrinsic quality in a work (especially in the ears of the professional musician), nothing more.

This discussion thus far has seemed to defend the teacher and performer from the accusations of neglect of contemporary music. The plaintiffs in this matter have indeed been guilty of loose terminology and of peddling some misconceptions. On the other hand, we teachers and performers most certainly do have some responsibility in this area, and it is true that most of us are guilty of neglect to a considerable extent.

Dealing with the Prosecution

To begin with, as teachers and performers, we need to take the responsibility for our own growth of knowledge in reference to what is happening around us in our own profession. Perhaps the element of truth in the case against us is the fact that oftentimes some of us do not make the effort to live as professional musicians of our own time. If we look at other professional areas, we would see immediately that to live and work even as much as fifty years behind the time would not be acceptable. Since music is a living, ongoing art with an outpouring of new musical thought being created every day, there is no reason to excuse any professional from making the attempt to know something about that thought. If some of us are totally encased in the past, either through lack of interest in today's music or the conviction that nothing worthwhile is being written today, then some prodding is indeed in order.

However, there is evidence which points to the fact that very few professional teachers or performers are actually totally wedded to the past philosophically. They would like to be more a part of today's music, and they try. The problem is that they cannot get their professional antennae adjusted to the point where much contemporary music communicates with them.

This problem of the breakdown of communication between the composer and his professional peers is one which has been often acknowledged and openly discussed, but there is but small comfort in the fact that this breakdown is for great segments of the music of this century widespread or that it has possibly never existed to the same extent at any other time in the history of Western music. Often throughout history, the *public* did not comprehend what a composer was saying at first, but with only a few exceptions the *professional musician* understood most of what a composer was saying right away. The music may have shocked or stimulated aesthetic disagreement, but the question of basic communication as to what was being said was not the primary issue.

Today in the minds of many professional teachers and performers, communication *is* the primary issue. The composer of avant garde or nontonal music does not communicate at all, and more conservative music communicates somewhat more in terms of perception but less well in terms of aesthetic response. The urging toward repeated hearings and more exposure may or may not be helpful, depending upon how much of the basic language of the composer's techniques is comprehended. To hear repeated readings of a beautiful poem written in a language one does not understand may awaken a feeling of general well-being, but an intense response to the poem cannot be experienced in terms of its meaning until one has studied and understands the language.

One sees repeatedly the attempt to grasp the meaning of new music fail in concert situations because the music itself is often enormously complex, of extended length, and of virtuoso proportions (both for the performer and the listener). We forget that, as we grew up musically, most of us gained an appreciation of similar works of the eighteenth and nineteenth centuries by dealing with the same styles firsthand through studying them at a less complex level. Thus we learned to love the B minor Sonata of Chopin — even long before we might play it — by having studied and played the easier preludes, waltzes, nocturnes, or mazurkas, as well as the music of his contemporaries. Herein lies the key to the comprehension of the large, complex works, much more so than in the process of repeated hearings. As professionals, we can deal directly with more complex new works in those styles with which we have become intimate through firsthand study. But in those styles with which we have not, we had best begin by taking the time to explore easier examples of the same kind of music.

Thus the process begins in our own studios, for us first and then for our students. Yes, the easier material exists and has existed, right from the beginning of this vein of twentieth-century music, right from such examples as the Op. 19 of Schoenberg down through music written during the past de-

cade. First, we as the professionals must study and learn whatever material we select. It is not at all advisable to pass it along
to a student without our own prior involvement. The reason
should be obvious: we have to understand the meaning of the
music and be convinced of its aesthetic value before we can
impart it to a student. We all know of students who are slow to
warm to a piece from the standard repertoire. We patiently
cajole, illustrate, explain in order to awaken the student's hearing and his or her response to the aesthetic value *we* understand
and know to be there. The process is exactly the same for new
music.

Having thus decided to undergo the baptism by getting
our fingers into new music (literally), we should realize two
other points. First of all, the field is far too large to begin to
encompass. So don't try to encompass it. Rather, dedicate a
small portion of your professional-growth time to it, and be
content to work as a student would work, carefully and slowly.
As with any large area, too much running about in an attempt
to gain a quick overview yields little or nothing in the way of
solid progress. Working with new music will be made considerably easier if we remember frequently that just as we did not
immediately understand much of the traditional literature when
we first encountered it as a student, so we may not grasp the
full meaning of the new music. With the traditional literature,
our teachers urged and reassured us as to mood, relationships,
and the ultimate pleasure to be gained from pursuing the project. When we now blaze our own trails, we have to do so
without the comfort of a mentor. So mentally putting ourselves
back in time to that point when our perception needed to grow
in order to deal successfully with the new can result in our
remembering to be patient with both the music and oneself.

In places where the music seems very abstract, dissonant,
or strange, it oftentimes helps to repeat a very small portion of
it — even down to a single harmonic change, a short melodic

fragment, a rhythmic motive of only two or three notes — until the recognition factor rises to the point where one knows what to expect. Sensing where even the smallest fragment is going or what it is doing can "bend" one's aural perception toward the composer's language enough so that subsequent writing becomes intelligible, sometimes suddenly and in much larger chunks.

Once having put forth a fair amount of honest effort, be prepared as a professional to pass some kind of judgment on music which you have really studied, and do not expect yourself to like everything just because it is new or just because you have invested time in it. We have all learned pieces which we do not keep in our repertoire — sometimes because we like other things better or we happen not to care for that particular piece as a matter of personal taste. With new music we run the additional risk of latching on to a work that quite frequently is of less than masterwork quality. One learns the music, plays it, teaches it, and if after a time one is convinced that its merit is limited, one moves on to other new music and drops the former from the playing or teaching repertoire. Such a procedure cannot be considered a waste of time, for one has grown in the process, and the music itself, even after it has been dropped from active use, remains part of one's experience and background. Such a procedure need not apply to all new music you work with either, for some of it may appeal to you so strongly that you will want to make it as much a permanent part of your musical life as your favorite works from the standard literature.

Finally, once having incorporated the process of dealing with new music into one's working habits, lay aside whatever guilt may have been whipped up by the accusations of the zealots. If enough professionals put forth a little regular effort, the best of the contemporary scene will eventually emerge in this age, just as masterworks have emerged in previous periods of history. Those whose interest in the contemporary scene is intense will probably always cry that we do not do enough; but we must remember that with today's communication techniques (printing, publishing, and recording), more contemporary music is available for consideration by more musicians than at any other time in history. In fact there will always be much more material available to use than we could consider, even if we devoted all of our professional growth time to it. And for most of us, time will still have to be saved for study of the more traditional repertoire as well. Our efforts to gain increased understanding of the contemporary scene should be constant and firsthand within the framework of the time we can allow, but the specialists will have to take it from there. Meanwhile, as our own efforts result in growth of perception, the range and extent of virtuoso achievements of the specialists will gain an ever-increasing professional following.

Part III

Transcendental
Studies

11

Mazeppa
(The Way We Wear)

*A*S musicians, we engage in an art which hopes to communicate something about our world and even, in its best moments, elicit both an intellectual and emotional response from an audience. No matter how much we become involved in the preparation of that communication, success or failure in the last analysis depends a great deal on the accuracy, speed, and refinement of purely physical responses. Yet, a curious contradiction attends the field of musical performance with regard to the matter of maintaining this physical aspect of our being.

It has been pointed out often enough that the human body is not a mechanical device and is subject to considerable variation from day to day or even from hour to hour. We have "good" days and "bad" days. We feel "on top" or "on the ragged edge."

There are, in fact, dozens of expressions which underline our inner sensitivity to this apparently mysterious variation: "in the pink," "under the weather," "played out," "in form," and many others. None of these expressions is used to describe long-term health or illness, but indicates rather only a temporary index of well-being within a fairly narrow gamut.

These temporary fluctuations seem to be hard to pin down to any definite cause or predictable pattern. Some prefer to ignore them. Others ascribe their comings and goings to various causes, such as astrological pulls, numerological causes, chemical changes within the body, rhythmic cycles through which we pass. The fact remains, however, that they are there and that all of us who perform are aware of the influence these states can possibly have on the efficiency of physical response during the performance itself. The flow of adrenalin which attends almost all performance can make us flush hot, sweat profusely, turn ice cold, sneeze, cough, become dizzy, nauseous, or suffer any number of other minor physical symptoms. These symptoms are often mixed in with the other body variables, and we often feel vaguely uncomfortable. Over and above this general state of affairs, the veteran realizes that most of the time this feeling of mild discomfort can be overridden, and the performer learns to deal with these inconveniences in the best way possible: by going on with the show.

Although we know this mild trauma may very well be a part of our profession, we surprisingly give relatively little attention to building up any kind of physical reserve with which to meet either the day-to-day physical variance or the stress of performance itself. Even in the face of a virtual epidemic of that bête noire of all keyboard players, tendinitis, we persist in daily habits which by and large ignore the most basic rules of caring for the physical organism. A large majority of pianists confess they don't take the time to warm up. For most, a quick scale or an arpeggio serves to check out the system at the beginning of a practice period, followed by quickly plunging into the rigors of learning or practicing the literature. We do not take the time to stretch and prepare our playing mechanism, nor do we sensitize our awareness to its well-being. Quite the contrary, when an occasional twinge of an ache or pain forces its way into our conscious consideration, we are very prone to push ahead by calling up an extra measure of effort. Some even rationalize such bullheadedness by invoking a vague connection between artistic achievement and pain or suffering.

If we compare these attitudes with those applied in other fields where accurate physical response under pressure is crucial, we find that our lack of regard for physical reserve places us in the minority. Look at the field of athletics. If someone goes "out for football" or "out for track," we expect that person to be undergoing a rigorous routine of general physical exercise in addition to the routine of specialized movements appropriate to the activity itself. We expect athletes to eat, sleep, and live in a certain pattern if they are "in training." They also spend a considerable amount of time in daily warm ups, stretching, relaxing, working out, and massage.

We accept the fact that dancers must give many hours every day to exercises which stretch and prepare the muscles for response, in addition to the special practice dedicated to mastering the choreography of whatever dance is to be performed. Dancers learn to live in a way, by and large, which supports the demands they must make on their bodies both in terms of daily exercise and dancing itself.

Every other practitioner, moreover, is very concerned about the physical demands of assigned tasks. Athletes do not attempt or recommend even fooling around trying to achieve physical feats for which they have no adequate buildup preparation. Dancers and singers are likewise sensitive to the physical demands of any repertoire piece. Keyboard players, on the other hand, are not the least bit cautious about attempting to

play big octave passages in pieces without having studied oc-
taves; etudes for double notes without understanding the special problems of hand-set, balance, or fingering involved, and
all kinds of speed and endurance challenges just to see how far
they can go. Others have the wisdom to recognize the cause-
and-effect relationship between such impetuous foolhardiness
and long-term or permanent damage. Conversely, keyboard
players often sport an it-could-never-happen-to-me attitude,
and they then complain with offended surprise and dismay
when they suffer a full-blown case of tendinitis and have to
foreswear serious work at the piano for a long period of time.

Unfortunately, part of the blame must be shouldered by
the teacher. Often students who are embarked on a course of
training for a professional career in music can go in and out of
studios for month after month without a word from their teacher about warm-up, diet, exercise, rest, or after-hours habits;
and yet, these factors may very well be determining ones in a
highly competitive field where strong nerves and physical
stamina play important roles. Often students are not guided
with enough insistence to stay away from repertoire for which
they are physically unprepared. They hate to be brought face to
face with the realization that their hands may be too small to
encompass physically demanding repertoire unless they learn a
great deal more about how to use their physical equipment and
spend time building a reserve of strength and endurance.
Teachers acquiesce far too frequently to the desires of the students with the vague sense that a student's motivations will
somehow make up for everything.

Furthermore, the very nature of our daily musical preparation is not usually conducive to a robust lifestyle. Unlike
dancers and athletes, keyboard players are involved much of
the time in activities which are sedentary. We sit on a piano
bench or a practice room chair for hours, inert except for the
highly complex, intensely focused activity needed to make music. Nerves are taut; certain muscles are in a state of highly

refined activity, while others must remain essentially still. Surely the strain on the entire physical organism is no less severe in this circumstance than that demanded by more overtly physical activities, and the fact that the activity is so concentrated and so focused into relatively minute responses suggests even greater need for attention to general physical activity and well-being.

Most music students are in a time of life where the body seems unlimited in its ability to sustain such effort. Health seems expendable. At a young age, one can live on junk food, stay up all night with a recklessness born of seemingly inexhaustible energy, and still manage to perform well the next day. The fact remains, however, that the successful sustaining of a career is an achievement which takes unbelievable physical stamina for years, many more years than the luxury of youthful waste will allow.

Life is not a table of rules and regulations. "Health kicks" are not particularly attractive to many, and overconcern for every small fluctuation in physical well-being can, too, become extreme. Each person must make many choices every day which add up to a personal lifestyle. Circumstances sometimes dictate choices which contribute to that lifestyle, and at other times they dictate choices which contradict it. Sometimes we even revel in exceptions, and from time to time many of us take absolute delight in doing something of a pleasurable nature which we know is not very good for us. So be it. The pleasure afforded by the exceptions and the delights, however, should not deter us from conceptualizing a basic lifestyle which we strive to maintain most of the time, a basic practice routine which is fine tuned to our playing mechanism, and a procedure for selecting repertoire which reflects our present stage of both mastery and strength. For performing musicians whose very art depends on precise physical response under pressure, that set of parameters should be very carefully planned toward the building of physical reserve and well-being. The long run will be well served by such planning.

12

Feux Follets

Charisma

*T*HERE are three elements that contribute to sustaining a career as a public performer. Each is important in its own way and each overlaps the others; yet we see each in varying proportions in the careers of the men and women who form our galaxy of performing artists. The three elements are *charisma, musical know-how* (including both the concepts of basic talent and development), and, finally, the *ability to use music as an art to express philosophical or spiritual values.*

When an artist steps before an audience, there is an instantaneous sense of life he or she projects, which is rapidly perceived at some nonverbal level by every person present. There is an interchange of something as elusive as an electrical charge, but just as powerful. Olga Samaroff, that great musician and teacher who worked in this country during the first half of this century, used to insist to her students that 90 percent of an audience would be definitely predisposed to liking or not liking a performer between the time an entrance was made on stage and the time the first note was played!

Charisma comes in many forms. Like physical beauty, it has many variables, but somehow the various elements must total into an effective, powerful presence. Without it in some measure, a person cannot in the long run succeed in sustaining a performing career, no matter how much work is invested or the degree of dedication, no matter how many competitions have been won or how many good newspaper reviews may be earned. In the last analysis, it remains today as it has been down through the history of public performance that some personalities are given the special gift of commanding a large public following and others are not. Even in those cases where the charismatically gifted perform less well from the viewpoint of professional standards than some of their contemporaries, the possessors of the magic will survive over the years in the role of the performing artist while the others may find themselves less well known.

This special gift when viewed in its entirety will contain strong personality elements. Lines of character will often be sharply developed and in such cases often produce definite quick reactions from fellow human beings. This interaction is the crux of the value such a gift has for a performer. It is also a two-edged sword, for there will be a certain number of people who are turned off by that particular combination of personality traits strongly projected. Thus, every artist whose charismatic appeal is strong will have those who secretly or openly express dislike and will wonder why such a performer has a following which remains entrenched and loyal through the years.

Appeal of this type is particularly hard to spot in students; but even more elusive is the fact that since it is based on some sort of instant psychological exchange — projection and recog-

nition of a social image which needs no explanation in words —
it can also rise and ebb at various points in a person's career.
For some, the strongest projection is thus one tied to the gifted
child. The remarkable combination of childlike innocence con-
sumed in the process of pouring out music, untouched by the
bittersweet quality of adult experience, and the expectation of
the bright future ahead have their own special attraction and
bring their own special warmth. At a later time, it may be the
full-bodied embracing of life by the youthful adult whose intensity of spirit seems to have the good things of life in abundance
at a time when living itself is strong and passionate. Some who
possess this appeal in their younger years may find it diminishes
as they mature; they change and are given no other image of
equal strength to project. Particularly interesting are those artists whose charismatic index has soared with maturity, often
with even middle or late years. These artists have often sustained a career over the years, on a less spectacular basis, on
qualities other than the instant appeal of this type. They suddenly find their index rising rapidly as they begin to project
such qualities as maturity, authority, and the simple fact of
having successfully met life's problems square on and emerging
beautifully with strength, wisdom, and compassion. For a very
few, a basic electricity, a projection of energy, or a love of life is
so strong that it seems never to falter during the aging process.
Change comes about gradually, kindly, and that artist is beloved
as a symbol of the various stages of life by his contemporary
audience, many of whose lives have been parallel chronologi-
cally.

    Charismatic intensity is not necessarily the same as musi-
cal talent and technical know-how. Probably the charismatic
gift is more rare, for although many have great talent, only a
very few in any generation are able to stand as a pole of this
highly charged interchange between performer and audience.
Such a position can seldom be achieved by hard dedicated

work, for although those gifted in this manner must work hard, they often end up getting tremendous response as a result of having done less work than many of their colleagues. True, some of the charismatically gifted turn out to be utterly devoted to their art, working with great diligence and endurance; however, others seem less so.

Neither is charismatic intensity the same as the achievement of consummate artistic expression or the ability to use art as a medium to impart philosophical concepts or spiritual values. Once again those gifted may or may not achieve the latter. Thus we begin to see that this most elusive of the performer's gifts — important although it undoubtedly is — cannot stand alone. It is the element which can add the luster and glamour to any career, if it is properly supported by the two other elements of the trilogy. For in fact, of the three elements, it is the one most likely to turn false, if left unsupported, leaving a dangerously hollow shell, glittering before a temporarily enraptured audience — but with the end result that both audience and performer end up feeling unfulfilled without really knowing why.

Thus charisma as an element is the most potent, the most exciting, but also the most perishable, and finally the most dangerous if left unattended.

Knowledge

Let us now consider the most easily definable of the three, the ballast of the trilogy, musical know-how.

The concept under discussion includes the initial aptitude for the perception of musical sound, the way in which this aptitude is developed, and the level of proficiency which is achieved to sustain the musician in his role as a performing artist. Obviously these concepts are the stock-in-trade of the teaching profession. We as teachers come to the point where we believe we recognize talent in a student, we believe we learn how that talent should develop (at least all of us recognize the signs of successful development whether or not it was under our personal tutelage), and we believe we can recognize the level of proficiency which is the key to professionalism in public performance. It is this aspect which is considered most directly by students of music themselves as they practice, compare themselves to their peers, and pass judgment on their elders.

Although this aspect forms the backbone of much of our music profession, most of us are quick to reflect on the fact that no matter what the cost to achieve the final level of professionalism, it is not by itself enough to sustain a public career over the long haul. This fact remains even when we speak of the *entire* concept of professionalism, including the *musical* aspects of the performance. Thus we have a host of absolutely first-rate musicians who are able to perform up to standards at least equal to that of the practicing concert artist, and on occasion at standards which even surpass those of more famous colleagues. Here we have the mainstream of performance being kept alive and well as an active part of our culture by musicians who are dedicated, who practice regularly, who perform in small concerts frequently, and who go unheralded by and large except for a relatively small following.

Oftentimes these musicians are happy with their role for personal reasons: they don't like to travel, they enjoy home and family ties greatly, they don't like the social aspects of a more public career. But aside from these personal aspects, the question sometimes arises in the minds of laymen, admirers, students, or even professional peers: "I wonder why he or she is not touring the world as one of the most celebrated artists."

The answer to that question is often of course an economic one. The person in question had to earn a living at that point in life at which he or she had the ability to begin a career as a concert performer — was prepared in every way — but did not have the means to sustain a livelihood at a time when traditional means of support (often parental) were normally coming to an end. At such a point in a person's life, other decisions of a personal nature (marriage, for example) point toward security rather than the long-term risk of building a career as a public performer.

But even quite aside from these practical considerations — which are often paramount — there remains the basic question of the relationship of this professional readiness to the overall prospect of long-term public success. Obviously such readiness must be there and remain the core of stability for such an undertaking. Yet without some of the color of the charismatic aspect, even the most expert professionalism can fall somehow short. Beautifully wrought? yes. To be admired? beyond question. Enjoyable? very much so. But all appreciation rarely transcends the limits of essentially intellectual evaluation. Excitement is created, the audience responds enthusiastically — but not enough of them as individuals have been caught up in an experience with such force so as to have lost their identity — forgotten themselves — to the point of not caring how this transformation was achieved; because to experience such at a nonverbal transcendental level is complete in itself.

A strong charisma, backed up by superlative professional preparation (both musically and technically), can achieve this phenomenon for a large segment of the concert-going public. Some of the fine artists who do not have this combination to achieve such a feat are indeed less gifted in terms of basic charismatic appeal. It is also possible, however, that some of them distrust or are even taught consciously to reject to some extent the gift which they do have.

We are all often properly taught that great art is by and large controlled art, and the very presence of charismatic interaction implies a high-voltage mystery and to some extent lack of conscious control of the overall scene. We learn in subtle ways to distrust this aspect of our gifts, and the long-term exposure by intellectual-academic tempering can indeed take the edge off such charismatic appeal. For any intelligent teacher, one of the most terrifying and difficult tasks is trying to help a highly electric, appealing youngsters find their control, gain their musicality, project their sensitivity without dimming the basic "animal magnetism" (Olga Samaroff used to call it) of musical projection. To achieve such a feat requires on the part of the teacher masterful psychology, constant ingenuity, and a healthy measure of downright luck.

Transcendentalism

The final element of the trilogy is the use of the art to impart philosophical or spiritual truth.

It is obvious from the start that the subject under consideration is one which is both highly nebulous and open to individual interpretation. Let us then begin by simply recognizing that — if we have been lucky — we have at some time been to a performance in which the artist, with or without charisma, became unimportant, in which the level of professionalism (the technique, the musicality, the sensitivity), although totally satisfying, was beside the point; and after which we came away feeling as if we had been given — miraculously and without having deserved it — a new viewpoint with regard to the eternal, profound questions which face every individual man or woman: birth, life, love, pleasure, pain, death — and most important, the meaning of it all.

Not every person will carry away the same revelation. Such extremely rare moments in one's lifetime tend to speak in those terms that answer the immediate spiritual needs of the individual. And yet in another sense, in a universal sense, the communication has been the same for each person who was thus moved. Each — the artist, the individual, and perhaps in some mysterious way the composer himself — came forth at a point in time in order to identify a philosophical or spiritual truth, which quite mystically can take on simultaneously a different meaning for each individual and yet the same meaning for all. Congratulations, accolades, standing ovations are quite beside the point. Those present know what has transpired; and for many, their testimony may be mute because they have no vocabulary to explain it. Or, attempting to explain it in a language of words falls so short of the mark that they refrain from trying.

Artist performers who are an instrument in this extraordinary event may or may not have charisma in the usual sense. When they walk on stage the entire matter of instant electrical interchange — of projecting an image, of poised excitement — is probably absent for the most part. But usually an audience knows what it will hear, so much so that instant reaction to the appearance of the artist is unnecessary (beyond a cordial welcome). It goes without saying that the artist who is to play his or her role in this experience is a consummate master of the instrument. (This probably — but not necessarily — means that he or she is an experienced member, and perhaps even a senior member, of the performing galaxy.)

Most important, however, is a philosophical conviction on the part of the performer that the art itself is but a vehicle for some other kind of philosophical or spiritual communication. This is a conviction that such an artist probably arrived at some years earlier in life. Projection of such a sense can in no way be a quick study. The artist must have lived with the concept, struggled with it, and given it the most extraordinary dedication — and discipline. Even so, we understand that no one achieves such communication on demand, that, in fact, years of soul-searching, hours of seeking technical and musical values, and the desire to communicate on this level may add up to but rare

moments of the kind of communication sought. Yet for all seek-
ers of such values, there is no choice but to dedicate one's total
energy to the possibility of being a part of a performance such
as this. As might be expected from the nature of such goals,
they may or may not be heralded. They may or may not be
graced by a large public following. And yet, the reward is con-
tained in the vision itself; the deep satisfaction is sustained by
the concept of the seeking itself. There is no other way.

Then, like a thief in the night, the miracle of using music to
touch others at the core of their spirits does on occasion happen. Perhaps the performer is not even aware when it happens
or in what measure, for the event is too consuming, and the
performer thrown too deeply into the special quest. But it does
happen, and when it does there are those who will be convinced
that art itself has achieved its highest cosmic function. And the
performer is no longer set apart as a charismatic pole; is no
longer the possessor of technical or musical attributes: the performer is all of this and more, becoming transformed into a
sublime medium in the spiritual quest of fellow human beings.

13

Eroica: A Call for Activism

AS musicians we are taught early on that modesty becomes us. Oh, there are a few of us who swashbuckle or act like prima donnas, but by far the majority of us feel that the very act of making music suggests we bow to the art itself, the composer, or the tradition, and the constant quest for a high standard of technical and expressive excellence leaves us psychologically in the position of feeling less than fully adequate, always striving, always reaching, never satisfied. The good side of this double-edged sword is that we continue to improve and to grow. The bad side, however, is that we are infused with an attitude of modesty, tinged slightly with an awareness of our inadequacies. This combination robs us often of the ability to sell ourselves to a larger market, or even to articulate clearly, when asked, what it is we have to offer.

To be sure, most of us can summon up half-clear images of

the arts enhancing quality of life, or the old adage that young-sters who "blow horns won't be blowing safes." But generaliza-tions of this sort tend to be too vague and shopworn to make much of a case for us. Furthermore, the aggressiveness and clarity which attends the rhetoric intended to support other areas of education — science and sports, to name but two — send us scurrying back into our shell of modesty, still convinced, to be sure, that we do indeed have a quality package, but also intimidated by the difficulty in articulating its virtues amid the clangor of the marketplace.

Courage to speak out is long overdue. We see our art relegated to an ever more humble position in the social order of our time. We see its finest achievements ignored, its intellectual discipline trivialized, and its expressive power sequestered. Few are willing to invest money or time in its appreciation, and an increasing number are unprepared to perceive its rewards. We suspect that in another few decades the wondrous form of hu-man expression which we love so much will be relegated at best to being regarded as an archaic curiosity and at worst to extinc-tion. And the body of evidence giving credence to these dark suspicions continues to grow.

Amazingly, we are still reticent to do anything about it. We retreat to believing with innocent simplicity that an ultimate justice will somehow prevail, because we know how good, how beneficial, and how rewarding music study truly is. We reason that it is, after all, so unlike us to be activists. We cling to the myth of a former time, somehow convincing ourselves that if we are but good enough, the world will somehow find us and discover our value. And yet we know that the odds of such discovery were stacked hopelessly against us with the advent of advertising, high-pressure marketing strategy, and a media net-work devoted essentially to developing a voracious appetite for popular culture. Furthermore, if we sense the need to address the hoi polloi and compete for attention, we feel somehow inad-equate to the task.

The time to throw off our lassitude, bury our insecurities, and become activists in the cause of music and music study is upon us. Each of us needs to begin to prepare for the most important performances of our lifetimes, the performances which will put an end to this demise and place music in the center of our cultural stage. The first step is to prepare ourselves to articulate clearly the benefits of music study. As we do so, we must be able to separate our roles as musicians and teachers, striving to improve our professional skills, from our roles as representatives of the profession to a larger, predominantly lay audience. We see such separation around us in other professions. Doctors or lawyers, for example, surely must strive for ever-increasing professional competence, but by the same token are able to turn a proud countenance to the larger, lay public and even close ranks rather spectacularly when reputations or vested interests of their profession are threatened. We must teach ourselves to react similarly.

As we identify clearly what our strengths are, we should outline them in such a way that their relevance is as broad as possible. We need to underscore the rather remarkable set of skills music study and music making bring into play and relate those skills to the art of living, so that they can be seen as highly beneficial to every person who comes in contact with music, not just those who are gifted, and certainly not just those who have professional aspirations.

Once those strengths are identified, we must practice verbalizing them, so that they are ready whenever opportunities to speak occur. Such opportunities usually come unexpectedly and fleetingly: a conversation at a social event, a question by a parent of a music student, a chance meeting with a business person or representative from the professional world. If the opportunity to speak out is lost, the ripple effect of enhancing our professional standing is stilled, and it is the resulting stagnation which damages our spheres of influence and respect.

As each professional musician thinks about the benefits of

music making, each will come up with a valid list. Here are some conceptual openers:

1. Music study enlists the gathering of information and refining of at least three of our five senses: hearing, seeing, and touching. For each, information must be perceived, analyzed, organized into meaningful signals, and acted upon. Perception which is both accurate and highly detailed is required for successful achievement. Such sensitivity is not always emphasized in our society, rife with casual sound, sight, and touch sensations. We are constantly surrounded by both music and noise not listened to, unwatched video screens running endlessly, and the impersonal touch of chrome, glass, plastic, or wood on handles, push buttons, banisters, cups, and wrappers. We begin scarcely to notice any of it. Moreover, this complex environment ultimately desensitizes us, so that we begin not to be able to listen, observe, or sense touch carefully, even when we wish to. Thus we are in constant danger of dulling our perception to a point where it is difficult to restore it.

Music study focuses on beauty in sound, not only musical sounds but also on counterparts in the world of concrete sounds, such as birdcalls, rainfall, or church bells (all imitated by music frequently), and on the response within us which the perception of such sound inspires. The musical page teaches us to use our eyes both to scan and to observe the smallest detail. And learning to love and to respond to the feel of playing an instrument or placing a vocal sound triggers an intimate sensory awareness, a tactile sensitivity almost unmatched in any other realm of human activity. Thus music study is one of the most powerful catalysts for strengthening and refining these areas of sensory perception.

2. Surely music study reaches virtuoso heights in the realm of abstract thinking. The properties of sound themselves — pitch, duration, intensity, and timbre — all must be conceived

abstractly, and each sound (with all its properties) must constantly be compared to the next. Structure in its entirety must be conceived, as well as the relationships of the parts to each other and to the whole. Whether dealing with phrases or sections or entire pieces, the mind is called upon to relate such things as relative position, importance, and function; and all of this must be projected against a time-based framework.

Such skills sharply developed by music study can be transferred to other areas. It is certainly no wonder that traditional associations exist between music and mathematics, music and philosophy, music and computer science (to name but a few), for these links are born to a great degree from a common utilization of and demand for abstract thinking.

3. Music thinking shows us how to deal with a learning process wherein physical response is an important component. Perception oftentimes runs well ahead of our ability to respond physically in a disciplined way. We have to treat the physical side with respect, care, and patience to get it to learn, but by the same token we know there are ways to work which will ensure that such response will be learned rapidly and securely. Music study is an ideal format with which to learn practice techniques, to sense the feedback from the physical side of the learning process, and to keep the response system in fine working order. Those who perfect these skills will understand how to approach any learning situation involving the physical, whether it be driving a car, typing, learning to use a computer, sewing, or almost any form of recreational or sports activity.

4. The relationship between making music and personal expression is too obvious to belabor. There are, however, a couple of observations which we don't always include in our thinking. One is noting the fact that almost all music making is a collaborative effort. Even playing or singing a solo is usually a combination of the performer's expressive inclinations and the composer's, or a tradition, or an imposed outline of some sort.

The degree to which that collaboration allows freedom of expression to the performer varies considerably from style to style. Determining the appropriate extent of freedom in each performance and the parameters of the collaboration are exercises which reflect the dynamics of many life situations both in the home and the workplace. Every music student, thus, gets a great deal of experience in how to handle expressive freedom, collaboration, and interpersonal relationships.

The second observation grows out of the first, but focuses specifically on individual heritage. Music as an expression of ethnicity is an obvious part of folk culture, but oftentimes this expression becomes muted or set aside as the quest for artistic excellence is pursued, especially if the art music comes from a culture which is far removed from the performer's personal heritage. This need not and should not be the case. One's own sense of color, pacing, drama, and emotional temperament is very much tied up with one's heritage. Knowing and understanding that aesthetic sense, as well as being very much aware of its interaction with the music, can only serve to heighten emotional intensity and project the music with deeply felt conviction. The process of recognizing and playing to these strengths will also build both a sense of ethnic pride in each of us and a sense of respect for the ethnicity of others. Music making can thus be a powerful catalyst for building this dual awareness, celebrating one's own sense of expression and appreciating its counterpart as it comes from others.

5. Music study leads to some kind of performance in most situations, whether for relatives, close friends, or in a more public arena. Often we musicians are apologetic or apprehensive about the stress and possible disappointment which attends such tests. As seasoned practitioners who have experienced the emotional discomfort of before and after a performance, we sympathize. As concerned music teachers, we worry about negative effects on our students if the stress or disappointment

becomes too intense. And we should. But in doing so, we also tend not to plug into a very powerful mainstream in our society, and thus we fail to note that we as musicians are able to offer all the excitement and interest which the larger public seeks regularly in its addiction to performance, particularly sports performance.

If ever a society was hooked on performance, it is ours today. All the way from Little Leagues to the Super Bowl, we revel in the challenge of performance. We perform in teams much of the time, but we also try to improve our individual performances in golf, bowling, running, swimming, and many other activities. We set our own goals, absorb our disappointments, toughen our resolve, try repeatedly, note our progress, and celebrate our achievements. "Personal best" is a concept we all covet, and it is born of performance. Moreover we see some type of performance in our jobs becoming crucial to long-range success.

With this type of mentality pervasive in our social order, we as musicians should be capitalizing on the fact that music making is one of the best training grounds for learning how to prepare for performance, for meeting its stress and challenges, for learning how to deal with both the short-range disappointments and successes, and for mapping out a strategy for long-range achievement. We should point with enthusiasm and pride to our built-in performance-training program, one which is virtually unequaled. We can do this without losing our sensitivity to the individual's struggle for excellence and can, in fact, become veritable gurus in developing a healthy psychology with which to deal with performance. We must, in fact, celebrate the performance component of our profession, and doing so will greatly enhance music's prestige in the social scheme of things.

An overview of these five skills developed by music and music study might look like this:

- Perception and refinement of aural, visual, and tactile information.
- Virtuosity in abstract, conceptual thinking.
- Ability to program and develop physical response.
- Expression of emotion and attention to balance and individual identity.
- Dealing with the preparation, disappointment, and triumph of performance.

Taken in its totality, the package is unbelievably powerful, so much so, in fact, that it has virtually no competition in any other academic discipline or human endeavor. Note again that the benefits observed are applicable to every student, not just those who are gifted or those who want to go into music professionally. Notice that the benefits begin from the first music lesson and continue working through every musical experience in the student's life. Notice how many times the skills we are teaching cross over into other life situations.

Once we have developed the ability to articulate this package, we will naturally generate an inner enthusiasm about our profession in such a way that it is contagious. Then be ready to take your positive, upbeat message on the road. In every community there exist many opportunities to share information which is educationally valid, and there is a great need for messages which are optimistic. Service clubs, churches, parent-teacher organizations, professional organizations all seek speakers who can inspire and point to values in the education of their children. The call to activism is an urgent one. It demands that our art and our profession be revitalized by those who love it and are willing to fight to see it take its rightful place in the social consciousness of our time. No one else is going to do this job for us. And if every music teacher resolved to prepare the message, to reach out in just half a dozen places in the immediate community over the next six months, the difference would be felt immediately, and the ultimate ripple effect could easily build into a tidal wave of recognition and support for our profession. The time and effort must be invested now in order to save our art, and the responsibility lies clearly with us — the musicians who love it.

14

Vision

The Physical

WHEN did it all start, this romance, this love affair with music? I suppose that for each of us the story is different, as it would be different were you to describe the circumstances of meeting someone with whom you had fallen hopelessly in love. For some it may have come in a flash: you heard a performance and something in the music left you breathless, perhaps with a lump in your throat, and you knew that somehow, this wonderful, mysterious substance would be close to you — intertwined within the fabric of your life from that moment on. Or perhaps it came on more gradually, like realizing that the person next door, whom you've known for years, is the person you want to marry. Or perhaps the conviction came as a result of months of study and pleasant, even low-pressure work; but then somehow you knew that life would not be worth much without being able to devote at least a part of your waking hours to working with music. However it comes on, you know that the presence of music will be there as long as you live.

Sometimes life will arrange itself so that temporarily you cannot work with music. Other things interfere, but there is always the gentle tug to return; and after the other things are taken care of, you always seem somehow to get back to that first love, never abandoning the desire to be as close as possible to the art. The years go by, and music and living are always there together, sometimes more, sometimes less; and when it is all over, those who remember at all will more than likely remember you as a person whose love of music was a guiding, dominating factor of living, as a person who was always devoted to this art, and even as a person who at times shared this art and was able to give pleasure to others through it. There is a famous saying attributed to Rachmaninoff, but any saying as famous and as universal as this one will undoubtedly be attributed to half a dozen authors: "Music is more than enough for one lifetime; but one lifetime is not nearly enough for music . . ."

Four aspects of the lifetime in music we are considering are the physical, the intellectual, the emotional, and the spiritual. All four operate simultaneously, of course, from the moment we first encounter music, but they are not always of equal importance in our thinking. There is furthermore a case to be made for the fact that the order in which they have been listed is the order in which they achieve paramount importance in our musical development.

The physical aspect comes first. In our early years there are ways in which the physical aspect is stressed — ways which are never again repeated. This is not to suggest that mental and emotional responses don't operate. Certainly mental powers give us the ability to direct our physical motions, and the emotional response may have been the key to our love of music in the first place. But as we begin to study in those early years, the physical takes on a unique importance; we must deal with hand position or voice placement, or how to hold a bow, or how to shape an embouchure. Thus physical control often becomes the first order of the learning process. We are, of course, consciously reminded by good teachers that physical control is only a means to an end, and we appreciate that fact in a way; still, much of our attention is focused on gaining these various kinds of purely physical refinements. In this process, one hopes for a certain kind of youthful satisfaction in the joy of just doing it, of being able to do it.

Remember how as kids we loved just to be able to *do* something, just for the joy of doing, or seeing if we could: walk on top of a stone wall, turn a cartwheel, reach something on the top shelf, whatever, we loved just proving we could do it. Oftentimes one finds the same attitude evidenced toward musical activities. A youngster may carry over that "can I do it?" challenge into the area of exercises and/or "technique," and when one finds such an attitude, it is cause for rejoicing. It is very likely that, given a normal set of physical responses and reasonably normal shape and size of physique, it is *this* psychological attitude which has more to do with developing a first-rate technique in those early years than almost any other factor. The youngsters who end up in their teens playing or singing way beyond their years are youngsters who have a history of deriving great psychological satisfaction out of figuring out how they can do something physical: hit a high note, play a hard passage, achieve a certain tempo. You name it, and they are ready to try to do it. And even failure does not diminish the job of trying, but only acts as a spur for another attempt or many more attempts.

It may be unfortunate that we live in an age that tends to regard the physical feats of the arts somewhat patronizingly. Virtuoso performance enjoys a long tradition in music, and the nineteenth century saw the rise of the piano virtuoso. Perhaps the initial excitement in conquering all those virtuoso problems of playing the piano naturally resulted in excessiveness. As a result, the pendulum swung sharply away from the adulation of virtuosity.

In the twentieth century one often hears sentiment which would indicate that virtuosity for its own sake is not worthy of pursuit. Perhaps we should reexamine this broadly held opinion. There is a time and place for everything, and the pursuit of a kind of hell-bent-for-Lexington virtuosity is a natural and very desirable part of the learning process. Indeed, it is quite possible that *without* the drive which is generated by this desire, one may never really push the limits of technical possibilities, and if one doesn't push those limits, one may end up with but adequate instead of masterful technical command. Like physical growing itself, there seems to be a period in one's development which is devoted primarily to getting this job done. And at that time, preoccupation with virtuosity can be not only exciting, but exactly right both in terms of developing what is needed and in terms of providing an important element at that stage for successful communication. As teachers and musicians, we might even heartily applaud this unbridled preoccupation with virtuosity — up to a point. This is not to say that with maturation, other qualities should not take the dominant role and supplant the virtuosity craze. We expect such a change with normal maturation; but in that youthful burst of energy we might as well join the crowd, enjoy the show, and encourage our youngsters to revel in the laurels of this kind of heroism. Probably never ever again will it be as important or as right for them.

The Intellectual

Meanwhile, intellectual processes will have begun working from the first perceptions of music. How heavy the intellectual will weigh in the balance of things depends in part upon the temperament of the individual, on how much the individual loves the pursuit of knowledge about music. Our age has put great emphasis upon the intellectual side of musical pursuits, partly because of its importance in the technological development that characterizes our age, partly because of a reaction to the excessive emotionalism encountered at the turn of the twentieth century in some quarters, and most certainly as a byproduct of the development of musicology and the ensuing respect we have come to accept for historical research. The technology of communications and historical research have, of course, developed hand in hand.

It is hard for us to conceive an age in which musicians knew only bits and pieces of what was going on around them in the rest of the world and knew hardly anything at all about what had gone on before them in preceding centuries. Yet, most of the giants of the eighteenth and nineteenth centuries lived and worked in exactly this situation.

Today, communication, technology, and research have combined to produce such a multitude of information that one might well feel inundated. Some composers, for example, have asked themselves the question as to whether or not there could be too much exposure to the past and to the activities of others around us. The question is not posed in the context of advocacy for cultural isolation. The benefits of being well informed about both the past and the present are obvious, but the constant acquisition of information about the past and present makes it perfectly possible to sidestep the challenges by spending one's time in assimilation, rather than coming to grips with the inner person in such a way as to begin to understand what it is one has to say. This point can be made whether we are creating or re-creating. There does come a time when the assimilation of new knowledge must temporarily come to a halt. All the knowledge has to be shaken down, evaluated, and let lie, so that it can produce the fermentation needed to generate an inner response to it. Notwithstanding this observation, at some point in our overall development as musicians, the quest for knowledge is indeed paramount, as it should be. This period often comes at college age. It is in this glorious time when we feel that if we can know enough objective information about the composer, the historical period, the influences at work when a piece was being written, the performance practices, if we can only understand enough, we are bound to produce the "perfect" performance. It is at this time also when we have little patience with any performance which does not square with our conception of perfection. It is at this time when the kind of playing and singing which was revered as being of the highest quality fifty to sixty years ago can sound dated in its details.

The perfect performance is conceived as the "ideal" which the composer imagined when actually writing the piece. This concept of an "ideal performance" which we must try to re-create is a very helpful goal. But the validity of such a holy grail can be questioned from a logical standpoint. We can ask, for example, whether or not a composer hears it only one way in the heat of creating? Or is there the possibility that, indeed, the composer hears it one way on one day and a slightly different way the next? Do we tend to fluctuate when we work with music? Maybe each of those ways is acceptable at that time, depending on emotional state and inner perception. The concept of the ideal performance gives us something for which to aim, and that is good; but shooting for an objective ideal also tends to block us off from a certain kind of spontaneity that can give vitality and projection to a performance.

Thus we have to remember somehow not to let the justifiable virtues of the intellectual approach take hold completely. We need the information, but to use, not to freeze. We need the thinking, but as the fuel for reflection, not necessarily to define the limits of imagination.

The Emotional

Now let us turn to the third category of focus: the emotional. Perhaps it seems strange that this aspect is considered *after* the intellectual. Is not the emotional response the first thing we sense? Whether in love or art or anger or whatever — does not emotion engulf us with its charged reaction, and *then* afterwards we try to figure out, or reconcile, emotion with the workings of the rational mind? Yes, certainly the emotional response provides a kind of instantaneous measure of our reaction to a given stimulus. But some philosophers contend that this response is simply a lightning-like calculator, giving off powerful impulses of reaction to values which are already deep within us and have already been perceived by the mind itself. Ironically, it would appear that intuition was being sought when discussing intellectual focus; and now that the emotional response is highlighted, values which were perceived by the mind and rooted deeply within our subconscious are being given credit. This paradox is important for us to realize if indeed we are to derive the ultimate value from all of the intellectual work of preparation which we undertake to do. To regard the emotional response as antithetical to the intellectual perception is to divide one against oneself. And conversely it is only by being very sure of the values one has chosen that one can release the emotional restraints, letting go without fear of ending up too far afield. A good example of this interrelationship can be seen if we look at the development pattern of those Western musicians who explore music of non-Western origin. Very few Westerners find that they respond emotionally to the music of non-Western systems. One listens — one learns a little about the theory of Japanese music or of Indian music — one even perceives and enjoys, but such music initially seldom reaches us in the same way emotionally that, say a Beethoven sonata, or a Chopin ballade, or a Schumann lieder cycle does.

Let us assume, for example, that you have a preliminary contact with say, Japanese music. You have had several opportunities to listen to it over a period of time. You may hear what is going on and thus have the intellectual perception, but no particular *values*, however, of a philosophical nature are attached to the sounds, and it is doubtful that a strong emotional reaction will occur. Several years later you have the opportunity to go to Japan. You spend enough time there to give you a real curiosity about Japanese culture. Over the following months, quite without reference to your previous experience with Japanese music, you find yourself reading about Japanese history and culture. You develop an appreciation for flower arranging. You begin to perceive, even if not fully understand sometimes, Japanese religious patterns. You develop a passion for sohji screens. Then suddenly quite by accident, you find yourself at a koto concert. It is quite likely that you will experience an emotional reaction to the music which was unprecedented and even totally unexpected. What had happened, of course, is that the values — philosophical, religious, and cultural values which had been assimilated over a period of time — had somewhere organized themselves within you into a recognition of what the music was all about from an emotional standpoint. You would be hearing the same scales, the same types of patterns which had been explained to you before and which had been heard before, but now you no longer even needed the intellectual crutch, for you would be hearing and responding directly to the emotional qualities to be communicated by those sounds.

This analogy is about as close as we can come to defining the growing emotional reaction which takes place in us to our own music, as we work with it throughout the years. We express it in different ways. We say that a piece is "profound," that we hear something new in it each time, even that we have associations of an extramusical type with it, and all of these things are true. But what is probably more true than anything

else is that music, in being written, was created out of and
linked to certain basic philosophical values of life, and our
having experienced enough life causes that music suddenly to
speak to us of those values. We ourselves have grown to be able
to hear the message. And as we hear that message, there are
emotional stirrings in us, deeper than ever before, stirrings
which give profound and new emotional meaning to that music.
Such maturation is what causes musicians to speak of the music
of a great composer, say, Beethoven, as having meaning late in
life which it never had before. Such music is at once terribly
personal and yet touches that part of us which we share in
common with all life and living. It speaks directly to that portion of our beings that has learned to identify with the greater
meaning of life.

The Spiritual

To attempt to put into words our spiritual relationship to music,
the fourth aspect, is a very difficult thing. Difficult, first, because words are finite, and the stuff of which we speak, the
spiritual, is infinite. But also difficult in a different sense because the age in which we live, like most other ages of the past,
has but limited interest in any sort of discussion of the spiritual.
A multitude of men and women come and go and never somehow come to grips with spiritual *values*. It is not that such values
are completely ignored or rejected. Indeed, each of us reaches
one or more points in life where we resolve to make the quest
for those elusive goals. But then those turning points pass. Life
manages to return to an even keel and pushes us ahead with the
pressures of day-to-day living. For most, the quest gets post-
poned in the rush. Oh, we all have a healthy curiosity about the
future, our fortunes, or our star signs. We all wonder if fate will
introduce us to that attractive stranger. We love knowing that

today is a particularly good day to transact some business. This is titillating and perhaps fun, but it has little to do with spiritual values. There is a deep-down nagging which keeps reminding us that the yearnings we felt at life's turning point, and even the fortune games we play, bespeak of a deeper mysterious reality. Contact with such reality, however, is difficult.

A multitude of men and women have testified down through the history of our civilization that knowledge of spiritual values does exist but is basically hard won. Such values are elusive to begin with. They resist direct confrontation and are better perceived obliquely. And although they can be developed and worked toward, such activity takes infinite patience, great forbearance; insights tend to be sporadic and fleeting, while the quest tends to be long and sustained, and oftentimes even bleak and dull. The great spiritual leaders of virtually all religions speak of the dullness, the bleakness, the black night of the soul. They speak of even the pain and the suffering — and of the fact that the quest has to become so all-consuming that none of this matters. Indeed, ultimately not even success in achieving spiritual elevation matters, but rather only the striving, only the effort, supreme as it is, only the longing and the yearning matters. Such longing and yearning brings in its process complete and abject humility, a loss of life as we usually live it. Then at that moment — in that split second, at the bottom of the abyss, in some totally mysterious way — the breakthrough comes, and once it has happened, one is never sure why or how it happened. Certainly one is never able to repeat it at will, but only to go on back to the yearning and the work and the hope that sometime it will become more of a reality. It is about such matters that Paul of Tarsus spoke of seeing through a glass darkly.

Indeed all of this can and does happen in the context of our musical lives at rare times. There *can* be a performance. . . . It is usually by a musician who has endured his or her own spiritual quest. And since these things are never able to be planned, such an artist — who unsuspectingly goes out to perform as reverently as possible, with as much emotion and understanding as possible — somehow during the course of that performance brings together a totality which takes on a meaning much greater than the sum of the elements that went into it. When or how it happens becomes unimportant. One only knows that there is a kind of communication which transcends all normal form of description. One is moved so deeply that one feels nothing at all except a profound sense of calm. One knows only that one is caught up in something so rare and so special that it may be given to share only a few times during the course of one's life. A sense of wonder and even detachment is all a part of the indescribable state that consumes all who share. And then it is over. . . . And when it is over, applause or display becomes an unspeakable vulgarity. We want only to depart in humble silence and to try to keep even the smallest glow of the warmth from the embers of so incredible an experience.

For saints, the means by which such transcendence may happen is through contemplation and prayer. But for us musicians, the means through which it is apt to happen is very definitely entering into the music itself. From this kind of experience, even if very rare indeed, we know that in some ways we have been most blessed, that we have been a part of a universal life force, that our art is more than a means of entertainment, or means of personal development, or even a means of communication of emotional or intellectual values. We know without doubt that our art is linked so closely to the roots of the universal mystery that it can on occasion put us in direct contact with the forces of creation, the very highest echelon of whatever order produced the universe.

Whatever it *is*, is so closely intertwined with our art that for us the two become momentarily inseparable, and in a mystical way our life *does* become one with music, and music one with our life.

Index